NO PATH i͏
i͘s STF

Celebrating
30 Years of Publishing
in India

Praise for *No Path in Darjeeling Is Straight*

'Parimal Bhattacharya's outstanding prose elegy captures the essence of Darjeeling, for me the Queen of Hill Stations, a place of many happy and sad memories.'

— MARK TULLY

'*No Path in Darjeeling Is Straight* is Parimal Bhattacharya's memorable contribution to understanding Darjeeling through a prism, where different colourful images magically come together to offer a remarkable clarity into the hill town as it once was, and its steady decline to what it is now. Bhattacharya's luminous prose and even more incandescent observations make this a mellow, heartfelt and evanescent ode to the town whose future hangs in balance!'

— FINANCIAL EXPRESS

'Parimal Bhattacharya metamorphoses mundane reality into strangely poetic and stirring experiences ... Succinct yet lucid, his narrative lures the reader into a mystical realm.'

— THE STATESMAN

'Mr Bhattacharya has not only mastered this way of seeing, but has also injected himself into this narrative, implicating himself in its fate. Consequently, it is difficult to pigeon-hole his book into a neat genre: It is not only a memoir, or a history, or natural history, or anecdote — it is everything at once, and more.'

— BUSINESS STANDARD

'Darjeeling has enchanted both laymen and the gifted. Only a handful, Parimal Bhattacharya seems to be among them, have attempted to see through the mist, as it were, in order to piece together an account that chronicles both the beauty and the warts of the hill town.'

— THE TELEGRAPH

'The memoir takes on the shape of a biography of Darjeeling, and this is so deftly interwoven with the personal that the reader does not notice when the book's two main protagonists – Bhattacharya and the town he remembers so fondly – switch places. The memoir is deeply personal, even when the town assumes centre stage.'

– *THE QUINT*

'[A] sympathetic and elegantly written account of everyday life in the Himalayas. It steers clear of well-worn tropes about the iconic hill station and the stereotypical views held by outsiders about its Nepali-speaking community. Instead, it explores the complex social and political dynamics at play in contemporary Darjeeling.'

– *THE CARAVAN*

'Part memoir, part travelogue, part amateur anthropology, *No Path in Darjeeling Is Straight: Memories of a Hill Town* is a fascinating and multilayered account of Parimal Bhattacharya's experiences in Darjeeling in the 1990s … [While it] remains grounded in everyday realities, it is not immune to the lure of the mountains or the town that is the site of nostalgia, memory and desire. This fine balance is the best achievement of the book.'

– *BIBLIO*

PARIMAL BHATTACHARYA

NO PATH *in* DARJEELING *is* STRAIGHT

Memories *of a* Hill Town

HarperCollins *Publishers* India

First Published in India in 2017 by Speaking Tiger
This edition published by HarperCollins *Publishers* 2023
4th Floor, Tower A, Building No. 10, DLF Cyber City,
DLF Phase II, Gurugram, Haryana – 122002
www.harpercollins.co.in

2 4 6 8 10 9 7 5 3 1

Copyright © Parimal Bhattacharya 2017, 2023

P-ISBN: 978-93-5629-006-8
E-ISBN: 978-93-5629-014-3

The views and opinions expressed in this book are the author's own
and the facts are as reported by him, and the publishers
are not in any way liable for the same.

Parimal Bhattacharya asserts the moral right
to be identified as the author of this work.

All rights reserved. No part of this publication may be reproduced,
stored in a retrieval system, or transmitted, in any form or by any
means, electronic, mechanical, photocopying, recording or otherwise,
without the prior permission of the publishers.

Typeset in 11/15 Adobe Caslon Pro at
Manipal Technologies Limited, Manipal

Printed and bound at
Thomson Press (India) Ltd

| MIX |
| Paper |
| FSC   FSC® C010615 |

This book is produced from independently certified FSC® paper
to ensure responsible forest management.

*For Indrani
and Isti*

CONTENTS

I   Home Weather   1

II   Dawn at the Butcher Shop   27

III   Salamanderland   43

IV   The Lights of Jorethang   73

V   Guiye and the Scarecrows   87

VI   Pemba's Umbrella   123

VII   Drumbeats in the Mist   165

Notes   193

I

HOME WEATHER

When the summer holidays come to an end, and the tourists make a beeline for the plains, that is when Darjeeling beckons me. July is the cruellest month here, July and August. The loneliest too. Weeks before the rains begin, as the heat begins to rise in the valleys, puffs of fog climb up the ravines and gorges to blot out the picturesque views until they are stretched out over the hill station like a grey dust cover. A dust cover for a toytown, packed and put away on the mountain shelf after the visitors have left, to be unwrapped again during the festival holidays in autumn. Until then, Darjeeling remains shrouded in fog, the tourist taxis with 'Sight Seen' painted on them are put under covers at Singmari, the canary-yellow cable cars are sent away to their hangars at North Point, the Tibetan stalls below the Mall fold up, the lodges and holiday homes are closed for the season, the Bengalis who work there return to their homes in southern Bengal, the porters at the bus stand return to their villages in Nepal, the Bihari shopkeepers return to their mulq. In the Gangetic plains of North India, it is the season of paddy-planting in rain-soaked fields. Not a sign of life is to be seen in the tea gardens after the second flush is plucked; even the livestock are herded away to higher altitudes to protect them from leeches. Rain falls endlessly through the day, the face of the sun cannot be seen for weeks and months. July is the loneliest month in Darjeeling, July and August.

The cruellest too. Endless rains seep into the cracks of brittle metamorphic rocks, seek out fissures, the ducts of dead roots, wash away the soil, and then, one fell moment in the dead of night, trigger a landslip that sucks in its wake buildings, roadways, trees, electric poles and sleeping humans. Darjeelingeys wake up on a grey, silent morning to discover that the scattering of huts on a hill slope that had stood there for so long is no more. Pieces of tin and wood are strewn a few hundred feet below amid a rubble of wet earth and stones. Limp, dirt-coated bodies are extracted out of it, bodies whose skins have turned blue and crinkled like paper. The survivors are given shelter in school buildings or in tents. In a few days, the remains of homes are picked up from the debris and the settlement rises again on another side of the hill. Old dovecotes and gateposts still stand upon the brown gash in the hillside, and perhaps a tin signboard that proclaims:

> GURUNG NIVAS
>
> BE WERE OF DOG

Wild creepers cover the muddy scar faster than the tears can dry up. Nature is fecund in the season of rains here; she takes life with one hand and gives back with the other in various forms.

Water is the other name of that life. Since the end of winter, Darjeeling pines after water like a frantic swallow circling the parched sky for a drop of rain. In March, the mountains turn a resplendent green, rhododendrons and magnolias bloom against blue skies, scented breezes ruffle the pine leaves, even the Kanchenjunga glows in the horizon all day long. Amid such a profusion of beauty, the townspeople are assailed by that most basic want: water. The municipal supply dribbles from the taps for a few hours every two or three days, unending queues of jerrycans are seen day and night in front of the few trickling natural springs in town, pushcarts loaded with jerrycans rush to far-flung neighbourhoods.

Fogs appear with the onset of summer, coils of vapour rise from the hot plains, the springs around Senchal Lake soak them up and slowly come back to life. But then, during this time of the year, tourists arrive in droves, Darjeeling's population shoots up manyfold and the scarcity of water doesn't abate. This vital want at the centre of daily life rankles, suspicion lurks in the corner of the mind, ears remain pricked up for the faintest murmur of water. Incidents of theft occur from municipal-supply lines, from private tanks; brawls erupt at public springs.

This continues for weeks until the rains return, until water flows again in parched springs, from artesian wells, from household taps. The gurgle of water swelling in the empty pot rises from a low bass to a rich treble and then brims over with a flourish. For the people of Darjeeling, this is the most enchanting music in the world.

~

However, these are outward features. The inner truth is, it is in the season of rains that Darjeeling returns to itself. Day in, day out, it continues to drizzle through murky fog, turning everything wet and dripping, and casting a film of moisture over every object inside shuttered rooms. The Englishmen lovingly called this 'home weather'. Viceroy Lord Lytton wrote to his wife in a letter: '... the afternoon was rainy and the road muddy, but such beautiful English rain, such delicious English mud!'[1]

But for the people from the dry sunny plains of India, it calls up a strange melancholy. A dull grey light from morning until afternoon disarranges the different hours of the day, strange mushrooms of memory and desire grow in the dishevelled depths of the mind, depression sets in. To these are sometimes added arthritic pains in the joints from old, forgotten injuries.

To battle the depression and pains is often more difficult than even facing the privations of daily life. Some give up midway. On 10 July 2008, a news item appeared in *The Telegraph* published from Kolkata:

Darjeeling, July 9: A merchant navy officer from Amritsar was found dead in a hotel room in Darjeeling this morning with police claiming to have found a bottle of 'aluminium sulphide' and a suicide note written in Hindi from his bedside.

Nardev Singh Mehra, 44, had been staying at the hotel on Robertson Road since June 29, paying Rs 250 a day. 'He used to bring food from outside and visited Mahakal Mandir, Japanese temple and Eden Dham in town. He used to say that he was writing about the history of Darjeeling,' said Bipen Sharma, the manager of the hotel.

In the hotel register, Mehra had said he was from the 'merchant navy' and had given his address as House No. 609/279, Royal Ludhiana, 1140001, Amritsar, Punjab.

The police also recovered a Continuous Discharge Certificate Cum-Seafarers' Identity Document, issued in Mumbai in 1993, which says Mehra was the son of Mohinder Singh.

Last night, hotel employees saw Mehra laughing as he watched [a] cartoon on the TV set in his room. 'He usually woke up between 6 am and 7 am. But today, he did not wake up till 10 am, despite us banging on the door and sprinkling water through the ventilator. That is when we called the police,' said the hotel manager.

The police broke open the door and found Mehra dead in his bed. 'We also found a bottle with "aluminium sulphide" written on it, along with packed food and a few banana skins,' said a police officer. 'This looks like a suicide. We are trying to get in touch with the police in Punjab. No contact number is available as he had no mobile phone.'

The police also claimed to have found a suicide note in Hindi. 'The note says he had been happy with his life and that no one was to be blamed for his death. It was pretty poetic,' the officer said.

It is always difficult to get to the bottom of an act like this. But there have been similar incidents in Darjeeling, and perhaps it is no coincidence that many of them have occurred during the rainy months. Ten days after the suicide of the merchant navy officer, on 21 July, a thirty-three-year-old Swedish social worker named Isaac Homgren hanged himself in an apartment on Zakir Hussain Road. He had taken the two-room flat owned by a Sherpa on rent. 'He had come here for meditation,' the landlady told the police. Three suicide notes were found in his room: one addressed to his parents, another to his landlord, and a third one to the government of India. It turned out that his travel visa had expired.

Wetness, depressing daylight and the nerve-wracking noise of the rains also conspired to cut short the lives of Englishmen who came to stay in Darjeeling drawn by the 'home weather'. This is brought home on a visit to the old cemetery in town, by Cart Road that leads from Chowk Bazaar towards Lebong. This cemetery was officially recognized in 1865, although there are graves dating back to the year 1840. Here rests George Aylmer Lloyd, the Columbus of Darjeeling, who first set foot in these hills way back in 1828 to broker a deal with the Rajah of Sikkim.

A few feet away lies Louis Mandelli, the Italian tea planter and ornithologist, who had a collection of a few thousand specimens of rare Himalayan birds. Mandelli committed suicide one dreary afternoon in 1880, although the local parish register was silent about the cause of death. Had it been recorded, he would have been denied a place in the cemetery.

In fact, there are a few anonymous graves outside the boundary of the old cemetery. They belong to the suicides. The unmarked blocks of stone strewn on the grassy slope could easily be mistaken as part of the natural landscape. The solitude of the place made it a favourite haunt of amorous couples from the nearby government college, and of drug pushers. On sunny days, children from nearby households would gather here to play tic-tac-toe upon the gravestones with pieces of chalk, women would lay out jars of pickled vegetables on the flat tops to sun them. The placid fingers of everyday life would close up the hot, open eyes of men lying under these stones for over a century.

There were fourteen such graves in the abandoned army encampment in Senchal. A sanatorium was built here in 1844 for sick and injured British soldiers. But, at a height of eight thousand feet, and surrounded by dense forests that remained shrouded in fog most of the year, the men became prone to suicidal urges. The base was eventually shifted to Jalapahar, the burnt hill, five hundred feet lower in altitude and on top of a ridge.

It is difficult to locate these graves now in the forest of tall conifers bordering what is still known as the Old Military Road. The ruins of a few brick chimneys covered with wild creepers still stand to tell the passers-by that men once lived here. The muted hum of automobiles on Hill Cart Road reaches up here through the stands of trees, to blend with the steady drum of dew drops from moss-covered pine branches upon the broad leaves of tree fern. A raven caws from a chimney top, a flying squirrel glides overhead, a spiderweb studded with droplets of mist glimmers in the shade.

What prompted these young soldiers to end their lives here, in this mirage of mists? There is no way one can know this, but the letters of ornithologist Louis Mandelli are strewn with the sighs of solitude in exile, thousands of miles away from home. Here he is writing to a friend, one Mr Anderson from Futtegarh:

> I can assure you, the life of a Tea Planter is far from being a pleasant one, especially this year: drought at first, incessant rain afterwards, and to crown all, cholera amongst coolies, beside the commission from home to inspect the gardens, all these combined are enough to drive anyone mad.[2]

And when Anderson wishes to visit him during the monsoon, Mandelli tells him about the frightful rains, horrible humidity and fog so dense that 'you cannot see a few yards before you'. It would be sheer madness, he writes, to try to undertake the proposed trip to Sikkim at this time of the year, because 'the leeches will eat you alive'. At the age of forty-four, Mandelli feels burned out:

> For the last two or three months I have been unwell and troubled with slow fever, cough, deafness etc., etc. In fact I think old age is creeping fast on me.[3]

Most of the great collection of birds and eggs that Louis Mandelli left behind, apart from these sad correspondences, have gone to the British Museum but a few specimens have found a place in the Natural History Museum in Darjeeling. Displayed inside glass cases, the dusty and faded snow pheasants, known as *Ornithocus Mandelli*, gaze with beady eyes at the small unframed portrait of their collector pinned to the green velvet backdrop. The cool, compassionate skill that Mandelli had perfected to snuff out the lives of his dear birds without ruffling a single feather was called forth one last time on a foggy afternoon in 1880 when he put an end to his own life with a vial of arsenic.

~

English soldiers were defeated by fog, neurotic rains and wetness that seeps into the bones, but the poor natives here have triumphed. Locked in an endless battle against privation, they hardly have time to lapse into depression. In a short story by Nepali writer Indra Bahadur Rai, the poor parents of a young boy named Kaley are fighting a bitter storm that is about to pull their tenement home apart:

> Again the wind began rattling the tin roof remorselessly. 'Clang clang clang...' it went. They feared the whole roof would be blown away. Inside, in the dim light of a lamp whose flame was wavering in the draught, Kaley's mother and father looked up at

the ceiling. The tin was blackened by woodsmoke, and in many places they could see drips like perspiration. Some boughs, as black as the ceiling, prevented those eighty or ninety sheets of tin from blowing off in the wind.

'How strong the wind is up on this hill! How hard it blows!' said Kaley's mother, during a lull when the banging on the roof stopped briefly, then she set about lighting a fire in the hearth.

'It's never going to stop!' said Kaley's father. 'It's been a whole week now!'

He had barely finished speaking when the rain began to hammer down again.

'When it rains like this I'm afraid of landslides. We were fools to come and live here!'

The rain grew heavier, its noise on the tin roof became deafening as a flame began to dance in the fireplace. They could no longer hear the sound of single drops: a continuous roar filled the room. Now it would wash everything away, they would be pulled down by a landslide that was sweeping down from above to bury them all.

It seemed as if the house was sliding away and pulling them down with it.

'Lord Mahakal! You are our Saviour and Protector!'[4]

As the tiny hut perched on the bare hillside is lashed by rain and storm, and the roof of the cowshed is blown away, Kaley and his little sister seek shelter in each other's arms. In the darkness outside, their parents hold on to the wattled walls of the shed to protect the cow. The family of four waits in the freezing cold for the night of terror to end. Far below, a torrent swollen with red muddy water rumbles through the dark echoing wood.

Dawn breaks to find the battered hut still standing on the hillside. Kaley's father sets to work on it, his mother goes to town to sell milk. As she walks about the neighbourhoods, comparing to herself the cosy life of her customers with the nightmare she suffered the night before, she grows desperate for a place in the town for her family. Her dreams are modest: a tiny room on rent, an electricity connection and a community latrine. For this she is ready to sell the tin sheets of their dwelling, and even the cow. She will sell vegetables in the market, and Kaley's father can work as a mason; even a watchman's job will do for him. It will be difficult to settle in a dingy slum after a life out in the open hillside, but her children will be safe, they will be free of the nights of terror during the season of rains.

This way a circle seeks to close, or a new circle begins to be drawn – the new, ever-expanding circles of urbanization in the Darjeeling hills.

∽

Work is scarce in Darjeeling for most of the year, especially during winter and the long tourist-less months of monsoon. Some of the unskilled workmen seek a raw livelihood away from the town on sparse hillsides: a flimsy tenement hammered out of tin and planks, a spring nearby, a tiny plot of land for growing vegetables, a cow or two and a pigpen around the stilts of the hut. These dwellings can be seen nestled in the green hills from the roads to Darjeeling or Mirik. Brown foot tracks peel away from the motorways and zigzag up to them, ribbons of smoke rise from the cottages, pots of cacti and geranium hang on the porches. If a passer-by cares to walk up to the wicket gate, a dazzling rooster might jump up on to the fence, flap its wings and let out a piercing call; a little puppy could bounce out of the balcony like a ball of knitting wool and yelp, inspecting the stranger from behind a screen of hair over its eyes.

The idyllic charm of these quiet dwellings is instantly brought home, but not the hardship and terrors of life on the isolated mountainside. There is the constant fear of landslips during rains, complemented by the back-breaking labour of finding sustenance from the heart of indifferent nature. The forests are being depleted, the springs are drying up.

If the nineteenth-century sahib artist who painted Lepcha girls fetching spring water in thick bamboo vessels could be brought back by some magic, he would find them doing the same chore. Plastic cans have replaced the bamboo, the ethnic dresses, too, have been replaced by jackets and skirts. Otherwise, they have remained as they had been more than a century ago. Keener eyes would see signs of malnutrition and uncertainty on their faces.

The romantic imagination travels to these distant settlements on swift wings; not so the health services, the immunization drives and census-workers, the teachers and the doctors. Life here is hard, death even harder. The sick and the dying have to set out on a long journey, literally, upon makeshift stretchers carried by fellow villagers along steep hill paths to the nearest motorable road and wait for the bus to town. Oftentimes life does not wait; its departure is not subject to the will of men.

Nor is its arrival. Ushered in by the local midwife or women of the household, it sees the light of the earth. The first cry of the newly born rings out in the hills like the call of a rooster.

I have heard of a ritual practised in traditional Lepcha societies. Moments after birth, the distraught baby would be taken to the village spring and given a purifying bath. The cool, reassuring water would put it to sleep and forge a bond with nature that would remain unbroken throughout its life. This way the baby would become 'mutanchi rongkup', the child of the community.

Most of those village springs have dried up; the few that still remain have dwindled and become polluted. The newborns are not taken there any more.

Sometimes the opportunity never comes. After the frantic screams of a woman in labour, instead of the feeble purring that is anticipated like the first tentative rays of the sun cracking open the darkness of night, a suffocating silence ensues. Then is heard a heart-rending wail. Fog rolls down slowly from the top of the hill like a shroud to cover the grief.

Infant mortality is very high here, especially in the remote hamlets. Shafts of stone placed in village commons or on the margins of forests bear testimony to this, not the figures churned out by government ministries. In the Human Development Report published by the UN in 2004, for example, Darjeeling was among the top four of the then nineteen districts in West Bengal where infant mortality rates were the lowest. What was not in the report, couldn't possibly be, was the percentage of births, deaths and marriages that went unregistered in the hills.

~

To escape these uncertainties of life, people flock to the town of Darjeeling in search of a home. Like Kaley's family. The unrelieved line of shanties along Hill Cart Road from Kurseong to Darjeeling screen the picturesque views – to savour which uninterruptedly the British didn't build a single tunnel along the entire rail route. Half of Darjeeling's population lives in slums. In the 1990s, after the Darjeeling Gorkha Hill Council was formed, the population in the hills grew by 45 per cent, which was much higher than the national or state average. The people who have come to settle here from Nepal partly account for this. Different political parties in the hills have, on different occasions, demanded the repeal of a particular clause in the India–Nepal Treaty of Peace and Friendship of 1950 that guarantees the free cross-border movement of citizens of the two countries. But the demands have always been rather half-hearted for the singular reason that made their counterparts in the plains of West Bengal turn a blind eye to the issue of illegal immigrants from Bangladesh: vote-bank politics.

In 1901, the population of Darjeeling town was 17,000; by 2011 it had grown to more than 130,000. Three thousand people are being added to the population every year. One should also take into account the seasonal labourers. And then there are the tourists: another 200,000-odd people at different points in time every year.

There is a fundamental difference here from urban growth in the plains. The topography of the narrow hill spur has made tableland scarce, removing any scope for lateral expansion of the town. And yet Darjeeling has been growing ceaselessly downwards, along the slopes.

On a journey here from the plains, as the vehicle rounds the sharp bend at Batasia, the town that leaps into the distant mountainside might strike the first-time traveller as a litter of junk that a King Kong or a Godzilla may have dumped from the top. Signs of decrepitude are visible all over the town that was built to accommodate ten thousand people. The life that festers on the edge of ravines, around the springs (read, drains), upon municipal septic tanks and hovels below Hill Cart Road is, for all practical purposes, a hands-on course in disaster management.

And yet, people continue to migrate from hamlets curled up in the lap of nature to come to live in the middle of this disaster. On a ramble about the narrow paths that twist and turn along the slopes below Cart Road, one would see flimsy dwellings being put together upon the smallest of perches gouged out of hillsides. There, Kaley's mother might be seen carrying stones in a bamboo basket, his father hammering out a cabin's frame with unseasoned pine planks, his little sister helping their mother to lay the stones on the floor, and Kaley himself might be seen perched on a ladder, passing the nails to his father.

Why do they come to settle here? What mirage of happiness wrenches them away from age-old ways of life amidst pristine nature?

A trek up to the top of Observatory Hill commands a view of the sinuous contours of the surrounding hillscape. Now brown and denuded, they were clad in dense forests fifty years ago. On clear days, a thin scattering of cottages and terraced lands are visible to the naked eye. They are lost in darkness as night falls, save a few twinkling points of light here and there. Most of these villages do not have electricity, piped water supply or a road connection. Life there has remained unchanged for more than a century.

What would the rhythm of that life be?

From a stretch of Cart Road above Happy Valley tea garden, a hill range is visible directly to the west; it is connected with the Darjeeling spur and extends to the dark green mountains of Sikkim on the left. One can discern the faint line of a road that worms horizontally around the folds of the hills. This is the motorable road to Bijanbari. After the rains, silvery threads of springs appear there. In the darkness of the night, tiny lights of passing vehicles flash like ghostly eyes, twinkle across stands of trees and light up the cuttings at the bends. From this shimmering line of the road, if the eye was to travel down the dark slope, dim clusters of light can be seen below. They appear like fireflies swarming around scented foliage. These are the lights of the forest villages.

Tuia was the name of one such village.

~

Pratap Lama, my student in Darjeeling Government College, was from Tuia. He stayed in the college hostel and used to go home on weekends. One had to catch the bus to Bijanbari and then undertake a short uphill trek to reach Tuia. But it was time-consuming, and also cost money. Every Saturday, Pratap would take a trail that rolled down across Badamtam tea estate, ford the river Rangeet and hike up to Tuia in about two hours. I was once on a visit to a school in Bijanbari as a representative of the government in an interview panel to appoint a teacher there. I searched out Tuia and went there.

It was a Sunday, Pratap was at home. The type of reception I was accorded on that unannounced visit, not only by Pratap's family but by all the village folk, beggars description. Let me describe the village instead.

Less a village, more a thin dispersion of cottages upon the steep hillside, Tuia, to me, was the sound of its name: the call of a tiny bird that plucks a ripple in the air and dies. There were about twenty cottages, made out of tin and pine planks, which belonged to Lepcha and Tamang residents. Old people dressed in striped apron-like garments sat on doorsteps, turning rosaries with slow fingers and offered the guest richly creased khadas which unfurled on their faces as they greeted him with smiles. Prayer flags fluttered from tall bamboo poles, orchids hung on moss-covered rhododendron branches, the crowing of roosters and the whack of hay being chopped were suspended in the air. Pale thickset women carrying baskets of cabbages and carrots on their shoulders flashed oblique eyes at the outsider as they hurried down a trail.

The narrow farm plots received little sunlight as they were on the north-western side of the mountain. The fertility of the land in these regions depends on its position with respect to the sun. A long time ago, all the fertile lands belonged to the Lepchas. They lost their holdings when agriculturists from Nepal, skilled and enterprising as migrants are everywhere, resettled here. This was also noted by historian Percy Brown:

> Before the advance of cultivation and with the disappearance of the forest to make way for crops and cattle, the Lepcha is in great danger of dying out, being driven away from his ancestral glades by the prosaic Nepali and other materialistic Himalayan tribes.[5]

The term 'development oustee' is a recent coinage, but the process has long been here.

Travelling on a mountain road, a cursory look at a distant village can tell you something about the people who live there. In a typical Lepcha or Bhutia village, there might be very little terrace farming, especially of paddy, and wild vegetation might be seen growing unchecked among tiny plots of land.

In Tuia, maize and some winter vegetables were grown on steep slopes. The strips of land were so narrow that cattle could not be used to plough them and the fields had to be prepared manually. But the fruits of such hard labour were entirely dependent on rainfall. The Rangeet flowed a few hundred feet below in the gorge, weaving a foamy green plait upon a bed of pebbles, but the water couldn't be drawn up. Electric poles had been planted before the last general elections, but electricity had not come. The poles stood at regular distances, covered with wild creepers on which violet flowers bloomed, like demigods guarding the unchanging pattern of life in the village.

In the government records, Tuia was a forest village. Unlike a revenue village, it did not have an elected panchayat, and all development activities of the state were supposedly channelled through the forest department. And thereby hung a tale of apathy and corruption.

Electricity had failed to come to Tuia, so had modern appliances. Time remained suspended in the dark, soot-encrusted huts made mostly out of unplaned wood from the surrounding forests. Most of the furniture and articles of daily use, too, were made by local craftsmen. In a settlement where nature and human ingenuity had struck an age-old balance, the only import from the outside world appeared to be plastic: plastic pots, plastic sheets, plastic pipes and plastic toys. The item that was exported in exchange was much more precious: youth. Very few young people could be seen around the village; most of the residents I met were children and the old. Grown-up men migrated in search of work. A handful of them, like Pratap, went off for higher studies. They never returned.

'Why would anyone care to live here?' Pratap asked me. 'What is there to hold us back?'

He uttered these words in a tone of soliloquy, as if he could see his own destiny before him. Then perhaps it struck him that it was improper to speak like this before a guest. So he took me on a tour around the village and to an orange orchard above it.

I had never seen orange trees before; they did not grow at Darjeeling's height. Most of the famous Darjeeling oranges were harvested in Mirik, Bijanbari and the surrounding areas. But at that time of the year, it was not possible to see how the slender, nondescript trees might look when the fruits ripened upon them. But one could always imagine.

In Andrew Marvell's poem *Bermudas,* there is a description of a paradisal garden aglow with oranges hanging on trees. Pratap had studied the poem in his first year of the English honours course. He smiled when I reminded him of the lines.

'Such an accurate description, sir!' he said excitedly. 'When the fruits ripen it appears from a distance as if the trees are decked with countless lightbulbs.'

> He gave us this eternal spring
> Which here enamels everything,
> And sends the fowls to us in care,
> On daily visits through the air.
> He hangs in shades the orange bright,
> Like golden lamps in a green night.

The oranges grown in this area gave local people much-needed economic support during the winter season. But their production and marketing were in the hands of people from the plains. At the end of the monsoon, when the trees would begin to blossom, these men would come to take them on lease; the owners themselves would become the caretakers of their own orchards. For the rest of the year, the trees would stand neglected and forgotten. I saw clothes lines strung across them behind the dwellings.

Darjeeling oranges are the messengers of winter, the favourite season of the Bengalis. They were the most prized fruits in the plains of Bengal until oranges grown in other parts of India began to flood the markets. However, the word 'farming' has always evoked in the mind of the average Calcuttan the picture of a landless Santhal farmworker bent over an endless green paddy field in alluvial plains. The picture of a Gorkha woman with a basket of oranges on her back has no place on the billboards of the ministry of information and culture. But the fruit appears in Bengali literature in unexpected places; in these lines by the modern poet Jibanananda Das, for example:

Let me come back again,
On a chill winter's night
As the sad flesh of a cold orange
By the sickbed of a person I have known

The sad flesh of Darjeeling oranges lies scattered by the sickbed of agriculture in the hills.

Pratap and I strolled through the orchard to a clearing that rolled up to a pine grove. Blocks of basalt carved with 'Om mani padme hum' were laid on the grass. The mountains of Sikkim and Nepal rose like walls behind the trees. Tuia lay on the slope below, its tin roofs glimmering in the oblique rays of the sun like a swarm of dragonflies gathered around a secretion of resin. Fleecy fog continued to rise from the gullies.

It was time for me to take my leave. Bijanbari was a two-kilometre downhill trek away. A car, arranged for by the school committee, was waiting there to take me back to Darjeeling.

'So that is your village, haan? What a quiet and beautiful place it is!' I said, and put my hand on Pratap's shoulder. 'Yes, sir. But there's another thing worth viewing. I'll show it to you in the evening.'

I protested. I was supposed to return to Darjeeling by evening. Besides, the following day was a Monday.

A bus left from nearby Pulbazaar every day at six-thirty in the morning, Pratap said. It reached Darjeeling before college started. He would accompany me in the morning.

Everything had been settled beforehand, it seemed; my excuses only elicited smiles – the trademark smile of Pratap Lama, Buddha-like, but firm.

'Okay, sir,' he said. 'This is the first time you have set foot in our village, who knows if you'll come again. Let's go home. If my mother allows you to leave, I won't protest. It's a promise.'

As we picked our way to the village along a steep trail through the pine grove, we ran into a group of charcoal-makers. Seeing me, they tried to hide behind the trees, but came out when Pratap assured them that I was not a forest official.

The group consisted of three people, possibly members of a family, though it was impossible to gather anything from their looks except that they were human, so completely covered were they in charcoal dust. Barefoot and dressed in rags, each of them was lugging three plastic sacks stuffed with charcoal. They stared at us with dazzling white eyes set in black, mask-like faces, and sneaked away down to the ravine.

They would walk on through the rest of the day, cross the valley below, ford streams and climb up to Darjeeling in the darkness of the night, Pratap told me.

Though contraband, charcoal was much in demand in Darjeeling to light household angithis, a type of heater, and grills in restaurants. Depending on the time of the year, a sack of charcoal fetched between two to four hundred rupees in the town's black market. But these poor men received only a fraction of the amount. The hazards, too, were great. The forest guards made life hell if they were caught in the act. So they had perfected the art of burning wood deep inside the forest and of camouflaging the smoke against thick fog by covering the embers with green leaves. Then there was the arduous journey across hills and valleys under cover of darkness. The juicy legs of chicken browned over the grills of fancy restaurants in Darjeeling had hidden costs; these rustic people were paying them. The forests were vanishing, the village springs were drying up, homestead plots were turning landslide prone. But poverty is an insatiable beast. Not only does it devour forests and the age-old systems of faith that have sustained them, it also feeds on the future of coming generations.

I tried, and failed, to get permission from Pratap's parents to depart that afternoon. That I would stay the night had been taken for granted; a couple of neighbours had been invited to dinner. Their hospitality was so spontaneous and yet so understated. Pratap's father knew the art of communicating the depth of his feeling with the hint of a smile or a fleeting touch upon the shoulder. Countless glasses of liquor couldn't spoil his poise and propriety.

But that was later in the evening. As the afternoon waned, Pratap took me above their house to a flat boulder jutting out of the side of the hill to see the most memorable sight of Tuia.

It appeared to be the favourite haunt of village children and idlers: checkerboards and tic-tac-toe games were drawn on the rock with pieces of chalk and clay. Tranquil cows grazed, stepped fields of maize rolled down, a gentle breeze picked up a murmur in the pine grove above. The light of the day was fast dying.

As we sat there on our haunches, one of Pratap's many uncles came up and handed me a tongba pot: a hollow jar of bamboo filled with fermented millet, and a slender pipe, also made of bamboo, stuck into it. I was asked to suck the pipe to imbibe a mildly fermented drink. After a few sips, the weariness of the uphill trek from Bijanbari faded away and a sweet languor suffused my limbs. I gazed ahead and saw the fog which had been rising from the valley all through the day shrinking under the orange light of the setting sun: it was as if a coven of genies were returning to their bottles. By then, thick shadows had lengthened over the village with surprising haste. The sun had dipped behind the arc of tall mountains along the north-west. Now the veil of fog was drawn away from before our eyes to reveal a truly amazing sight. Before us, at a distance of about five kilometres as the crow flies, Darjeeling town lay upon the narrow spur. Fog had kept it hidden during the day, but now it seemed to dominate the eastern horizon. Countless windowpanes and the tin roofs of miniature houses glinted in the light of the setting sun. I could never have imagined how unbelievably congested and bereft of green Darjeeling was if I had not seen it like this. Dark threads of roads twisted across packed blocks of buildings, antlike vehicles scurried upon them. A ribbon of smoke rose above the railway station to the right; below it, the blue dome over the palace of the Maharaja of Burdwan glowed. A Z-shaped track cut across the dark green face of Happy Valley tea garden.

Pratap and I improvised a game. He would name a well-known building of the town and I would search it out from the dense, bristling urban forest. Then we would switch. Together, we found Bishop House, Loreto Convent, St Joseph's College, St Andrew's Church, Windermere Hotel, Ajit Mansions, the staff quarters of the government college, Cozy Café ... This continued until daylight died, until evening settled over Tuia with the lowing of cows, the faint wail of a baby and the barking of dogs. As we began to climb down from the rock terrace, the lights of Darjeeling had come on.

While the bright lights glowed across the sky like silent fireworks, kerosene lamps glimmered here and there in Tuia. Together, they created an uneasy spell, a confused feeling that cannot be described in language, one that builds up in the chest like stifled sighs. The more the darkness deepened, the more the lights of Darjeeling brightened, their radiance buzzed in the inky sky like a beehive.

We came to sit upon the broad wooden porch in Pratap's house. Two guests from the neighbourhood had already arrived; the male members of the extended household were also present. We struck up a conversation – they in broken Hindi and I in my pathetic Nepali. Guraans, a homemade liquor distilled from rhododendron petals, was poured into glasses and plates heaped with bhuteko masu – mutton fried with lots of garlic and red chillies – were passed around. The starry lights of Darjeeling glowed on the distant horizon.

Suddenly I noticed something: perhaps it was a coincidence, but while all the elderly men had their backs turned to the glittering townscape, the relatively young ones sat facing it.

I was introduced to Rupen, Pratap's young cousin, who was standing away from the circle of conversation. He was studying in Class 11 at North Point School in Darjeeling and had a passion for music. Rupen smiled bashfully when I asked him to sing something for us, but gave in at the urgings of the womenfolk and fetched his guitar.

Of the three or four songs that Rupen sang that evening, one was Harry Belafonte's 'Jamaica Farewell'; the rest were contemporary rock. I have heard 'Jamaica Farewell' so many times on so many different occasions, but listening to the song that evening in the sleepy hamlet nestled in the wooded hills was an unforgettable experience. Rupen sang with deep absorption, standing with his back against the railing and keeping the beat with his feet on the wooden floor. I learnt that he was yet to see the sea with his own eyes. But the magic cast by his voice transformed the veranda into the deck of a Caribbean ship, raring to set out upon uncharted seas.

Another song that he sang that evening, one by a Western rock group named Bloodkin, had a haunting lyric whose first few lines became etched in my memory.

> Who do you belong to?
> I'm sure it's not yourself
> Who do you sing love songs to?
> 'Cause you sing 'em all day long –
> But that's not your voice
> Not as far as I can tell

As he plucked the strings of the guitar and shook his head, Rupen's eyes wandered into the distance where Darjeeling lay like fistfuls of iridescent gems upon black velvet.

~

For more than a century, hill people from far and wide were attracted like flying insects by the lights of Darjeeling. Their stories are strewn around every bend in the roads of the town. These are stories of pluck and prosperity, of leaving the stagnant life of their villages and of survival against the odds of an expensive hill station. But that is not all. The stories of failure and loss, of trickery and broken hearts, can be found in sad taverns of remote hamlets, in bitter glasses of raksi and in tattered shoes propped up on lonely cottage steps.

The fairytale of Darjeeling is woven out of these two kinds of stories. Indra Sundas's short story 'Sainlo' is about a hillbilly who comes to town:

Sainlo was a villager of Halesi in Nepal. He had heard alluring talks about Darjeeling, then commonly known as Gundribazaar. Unable to resist the temptation, he fled from the byre of his master and joined a group of villagers who were bound for Assam to earn their livelihood. Although he had to go on foot for a number of days, he did not feel tired. His sound health and his eagerness to see Darjeeling sustained him on the way, and fatigue could not overpower him at all. Passing Simana, Suke and Ghoom, he, along with others, arrived at Gundribazaar. On the way, he saw strange villas and cottages, Jangbir's artistic waterspouts with a pavilion, the railway station, the railway tracks, motor vehicles and other objects of interest which amazed him. The delectable sight made him feel that he had reached heaven.[6]

Sainlo never returned to his village. With the help of an avuncular local merchant, he became a cart-driver who transported charcoal and firewood from nearby forest tracts. On dark, freezing nights, Sainlo's raucous voice could be heard from afar, above the steady groan of cartwheels. One foggy night he saw ghosts on a deserted stretch of the road. The following morning the cart was found by the roadside, upturned, with Sainlo and the two bullocks lying dead beside it.

Sainlo's sad story has the shape of a fable. A long journey that begins in a remote village in Nepal ends finally in the fatal mirage of Darjeeling.

II

DAWN AT THE BUTCHER SHOP

Like Sainlo, I too was drawn by the enchantment of Darjeeling. It was the beginning of the 1990s, the agitation in the hills had just ended. I went there with a letter of appointment to a college teacher's job in my pocket. This was my first visit. Naturally, I was excited.

But my mother was not. Shadows of anxiety had gathered over her face since my interview at the office of the Public Service Commission.

'What madness! Aren't there teaching jobs elsewhere that you have to risk your life to go there?' my mother said, her chin propped on her cupped palm like Apu's mother Sarbajaya in Satyajit Ray's *Aparajito*.

There really was no teaching job available at the time. Recruitments in colleges and universities had been stalled following a controversy over the mandatory National Eligibility Test for teachers. The tenure of my research fellowship, on the other hand, was nearing its end. A lectureship in a government college was, for me, like the last metro in a midnight city.

'Don't be silly, Ma,' I said. 'People are going to Darjeeling every day. Are they getting killed?'

'Have you forgotten those newspaper reports?' Mother retorted. 'They even shot at the SP.'

'But those days are past, things are returning to normal since the peace accord was signed.'

'Maybe. I don't know,' she said resignedly. 'But you wouldn't understand what passes through the mind of a mother when her son decides to go to work in such a dangerous place.'

I could vaguely sense the shape of her anxiety, her fear of the unknown. Though very much within the state, and only 623 kilometres from Calcutta, Darjeeling was, to average Bengalis, for all practical purposes, a remote and exotic place. The same element that evoked its irresistible romance had instilled in my mother an ineffable fear.

The person who was ready to exchange this fear for the romance was Dadu, my grandfather. He was enthralled by the news of my appointment.

What kind of a person was Dadu?

If her anxious attachment to the son made my mother resemble Sarbajaya in Ray's *Aparajito*, then Dadu would surely have been the headmaster in the film. He had the same short, erect frame, the Hitleresque moustache, the same obsession with primness and punctuality. The frame had sagged in the autumn of his life, the moustache, too, had greyed, but his manners had remained intact. He had retired as a postmaster in a district town, but he could as well have been a stationmaster, a wardmaster or any type of master who were the indispensable cogs in the wheel of the British Empire. His professional life had been filled with the thud of letter bags, the rattle of the telegraph and the bang of seal hammers, but there would always be Shakespeare and Browning, Carlyle and Chesterton lurking under the toothbrush moustache. As a matter of fact, Dadu was a pucca sahib trapped in the body of a Bengali babu, an Anglican Christian encased in an orthodox Brahmin. Nesfield's grammar book was his Bible, *The Statesman* his daily psalm book. His favourite poet was Wordsworth and his favourite flower was the daffodil, though he had never set his eyes on one. But daffodils bloomed in Wordsworth's poetry, and that was enough for him.

In the early 1940s, Dadu had visited Darjeeling as a government witness in a money order forgery case and stayed there for a fortnight. That experience had grown roots in his memories. There was an unframed photograph of him in his bookcase, propped up against *Roget's Thesaurus*; it showed a young man standing against the background of a pine grove wearing a dhoti, a serge jacket, long woollen socks, boots and a pair of pince-nez clasped upon his nose. Mists of time had left yellow splotches on the photograph.

The appointment letter took time to reach me through the dusty labyrinth of the Directorate of Higher Education. My days of waiting began to fill up with Dadu's reminiscences of an enchanting town whose air was forever redolent with the smell of walnut cakes and forever echoing with the strains of the Gorkha regimental band, whose winding paths were dotted with red-roofed cottages and stands of deodars: all these bathed in the warm glow emanating from Wordsworth's Lake District and Thomas Hardy's Wessex. When, at last, I boarded the Darjeeling Mail at Sealdah station on a muggy July evening, the state of my mind was like that of Sainlo, the ox-cart driver in Indra Sundas's story.

~

Dadu, too, had travelled by Darjeeling Mail. It was the fastest and most luxurious train in those days. In the evening, half an hour before its scheduled departure, a bevy of Austins, Fords, John Morrises, Chevrolets and a couple of Rolls-Royces would pull up at the driveway adjacent to platform number 9 at Sealdah station. There would be no rush, no scramble, no noisy din. Pairs of sahib-mems would pace down the platform arm in arm, their babalog in tow holding the hands of ayahs, followed by servants and coolies laden with luggage. The drivers and guards were all Anglo-Indians – called Eurasians in those days. The first-class passengers were served a four-course dinner in well-furnished dining cars and premium Darjeeling tea at dawn. After the river crossing, another train would take them to

Siliguri station sharply at five past six in the morning. There, waiting on the other side of the platform, would be the fairytale narrow-gauge train; its blue toy engine, emblazoned with the logo of Messrs Sharpe, Stewart and Co. of Glasgow, packing steam in its boiler. The romance of Darjeeling would commence from here.

Fifty years later, on a wet July morning, there was not a shred of romance at the Tenzing Norgay Bus Terminus in Siliguri. No crowd of tourists, no restless queues at the ticket counters – it was the off season. A beat-up Willys jeep with a grimy tarpaulin hood was revving its engine, waiting to fill up the two remaining seats at the back. The driver's assistant, a young man with Mongolian features, stood with his elbows propped against the bonnet and yodelled: 'Dhorhzeling! Dhorhzeling! Dhorhzeling!' A black leather jacket hung across his shoulders and a red golf cap sat askew upon his head. All the passengers were from the hills. They had come to Siliguri earlier in the morning on sundry errands and were now patiently waiting inside the jeep to escape the sticky heat of the plains. The vehicle's roof had been piled high with boxes and sacks, and half a dozen red plastic chairs with legs raised up against the grey, cloudy sky. I was given a seat between a young man and a middle-aged woman with a newly plastered arm.

As the jeep untangled itself from the mess of traffic on the roads of Siliguri and turned right at Darjeeling More, I had my first view of the mountains – a bluish-black wall stretched across the distant horizon, its crest lost in charcoal-grey clouds. Scenes from a shanty town appeared on the wayside: dwellings of tin and wood, children playing, pigs rooting about, lines of trucks, automobile repair shops, dhabas and pice hotels. And then, suddenly, taut and straight as the strings on a violin, the road went through emerald-green tea gardens that fanned out like an overture in C minor. We entered the shaded plantation of tall sal trees. There were the lumberyards, the forest bungalow and the pretty little station of the Darjeeling Himalayan Railway – Sukna.

Sukna means dry. In the damp, miasmal belt of the Terai forests in the Himalayan foothills, this was a rare dry spot that the British found where they had built a bungalow for game hunting. In those days, the jungle teemed with animals – wild boars, elephants, deer, nilgai, rabbits, and also a large population of leopards and tigers. The train carrying my grandfather to Darjeeling had halted at Sukna to fill water in its engine. A young man about my age then, he had stepped out on to the platform and spotted a pair of large grey rabbits a couple of yards away on a grassy plot.

Years before, on a bright winter morning in 1900, a huge tiger was found basking in the sun in front of the stationmaster's room. The train was detained. Incidentally, a hunter was lodging in the nearby forest bungalow. He rushed to the spot and dispatched the beast. Again, in February 1915, the train's noise had roused a big cat napping under a culvert. Greatly peeved, the king of the jungle had charged at the metal beast rolling on wheels. Such incidents were not uncommon, and herds of wild elephants blocking the track were a regular feature. Blasts of the whistle and steam would drive them away.

Since the beginning of time, the Terai belonged to these denizens of the forest; they never accepted the intrusion of men. In fact, it was these animals, and not the indigenous people, who had put up a stiff resistance against colonial expansionism. And in this fight, a species of tiny winged insect was far more intrepid than the big cats and elephants. This was the mosquito, *Anopheles fluviatilis*. Shadows of inscrutable death hung in the foetid, sunless depths of this forest belt, especially before Ronald Ross's discovery of the malarial parasite carried by the mosquito. Travellers to Darjeeling hastened to cross this region as quickly as possible.

But it was impossible for the miniature train to pick up a speed of more than ten miles per hour, now that it had left the flat plains and was crawling up the hill slope. On the right there would be thick growths of moss and fern upon the cutting, so close to the windows that they often kissed the passengers on their cheeks, while on the left would be visible deep ravines with birds flitting about over the tangled canopies of trees. The nature of the forest would begin to change from here.

As L.S.S. O'Malley, an Indian Civil Service officer who compiled a number of gazetteers of the Bengal province in the first two decades of the twentieth century, writes in the Darjeeling district gazetteer: 'there are, in fact, probably few places in the world in which so many different types of forest exist within so small an area.'[1] Joseph Dalton Hooker's *Himalayan Journals*, too, is filled with a sense of awe at the diversity of flora here. The forest of robust sals, *Shorea robusta*, began in Sukna and ended near Rongtong; they are scarce above three thousand feet. Other than the altitude, a type of soil in this part of the Terai plays a role in the growth of this tree species, a great favourite of the British engineers for their use as sleepers on railways tracks. The clean staccato notes of sal-wood sleepers under the carriage wheels added charming music to railway travels of yore.

Now one would see tall tuns, *Toona ciliata*, that had lent their name to the tiny rail station, Tung. And then, at around four thousand feet, maples, birches, alders and piplis would drift into view. Thickets of slender bamboos, chestnuts, magnolias and laurels would be seen at six thousand feet. Time was when these trees added to the picturesque charm of Darjeeling, but they have been pushed to the margins ever since the cryptomeria pines were imported from Japan. Further up, rhododendrons would appear, and then, above eight thousand feet, the majestic silver firs would tower with their tinfoil foliage.

Eighteen kilometres from Siliguri town, after the first of a series of loops on the railway track is passed, comes the sleepy hamlet of Rongtong. It has a railway station. Once upon a time, there was a dense forest here infested with leopards. More than sixty of them, twice in pairs, had been trapped in a steel cage set up by the public works department that Dadu had seen from the train. Some of their skins still hang on the walls of the tea-garden bungalows here.

~

I didn't see the cage. The forest had disappeared, the sinuous hills were draped in the monotonous green of the tea gardens, gashed in places with brown landslips. Far below, the teak plantations of Sukna were dusted with a pale yellow bloom. Thin mist crept over them to shade into the haze of Siliguri town in the horizon. Had Dadu seen this, he would surely have recited to himself the lines from his favourite poet:

> This City now doth, like a garment, wear
> The beauty of the morning; silent, bare,
> Ships, towers, domes, theatres, and temples lie
> Open unto the fields, and to the sky;
> All bright and glittering in the smokeless air

But my head felt heavy, my stomach turned. Our vehicle had stopped beside a tea stall perched on the edge of a deep ravine. All the passengers except I and the lady with the plastered arm got off to have tea. The young man sitting beside me had noticed the signs of discomfort on my face. He came forward and said in Hindi, 'Why don't you have a cup of tea? It'll make you feel better.'

The stall was made of rough wooden planks nailed together and painted a garish red with Coca-Cola advertisements. A pair of petite slit-eyed women, either siblings or mother and daughter, were briskly selling tea, momos and a type of doughnut. One of them asked me, 'Tapai lai ke diun?'

The young man ordered tea for both of us and took me inside the shop. Red plastic chairs were arranged around red plastic tables there. Tea was served in squat steel tumblers. We began to chat as we sipped milky, oversweet tea and, surprisingly, I began to feel better.

The young man owned a chemist's shop in Sonada. When I told him the purpose of my journey, he warmed to me instantly and said that he was an alumnus of Darjeeling Government College. It turned out that he had passed out of college a year before I myself did. His name was Nikhil Tamang.

Agile and affable, Nikhil Tamang was my first acquaintance in the Darjeeling hills. Over time, I would meet many people and become close with some of them, but the warmth of that first meeting with Nikhil is still alive in my memory after all these years. Since that day, every time I would pass his shop in Sonada Bazaar on my way to and from Darjeeling, I would wave my hand and he would respond with a beaming smile and a bow. Nikhil's smiles helped me fend off the dejection of return after visits home and brought the alien hills a little closer to my heart. Over the next few years, a bend in the road, the shape of a rock, a dog at the Kurseong bus stand, a sisu tree at Longview tea estate whose trunk resembled a tusker, the charms of a Lepcha woman who sold fresh vegetables at Ghaiyabari, and other objects of interest were etched in my memory and made the long hill road to Darjeeling as intimate as a line on the palm of my hand. But that first journey was filled with the anxiety of the unknown. It was devoid of the romance Dadu had known.

∼

In fact, the Darjeeling Himalayan Railway is a romance, a courtship between the mountains and a feat of engineering, between indomitable nature and colonial enterprise. In a song sequence from the Hindi film *Aradhana*, shot in Darjeeling, where Rajesh Khanna, from a hoodless jeep, serenades Sharmila Tagore sitting at the toy train's window – with 'Mere sapnon ki rani kab ayegi tu' – their courtship is matched by that of the automobile and the locomotive running in tandem, and also the courtship of the railway track and the Hill Cart Road. Above Rongtong, the train traverses the third loop on the track and halts at the station of Chunabhatti, which means lime quarry. Limestone found here was used in the Tudor-style buildings of Darjeeling and Kurseong. After Chunabhatti, the climb becomes steeper, and here begins the first of the famous reverses. The train reverses a few metres on a branching track along an incline and then hurtles forward full steam and is propelled up the rise.

There is an apocryphal story that the engineer assigned to the construction of this segment of the railway was struggling to align the track with the steep gradient here. The work was getting delayed; plans were afoot to scrap the blueprint and begin a new survey. This would have meant further delay and a longer absence of the engineer from home. So it was his wife who chipped in; she hit upon the idea of a reverse track. In a ball dance, if a couple inadvertently veered to a corner of the room, it was customary for one of them to move back one step, take two steps forward and return to the centre of the floor. If such an exigency was permitted even at the viceroy's ball, then why not on a difficult railway track, she had argued. It was a toy train after all!

And thus was born the wonderful reverse in the Darjeeling Himalayan Railway.

The train would waltz along the winding mountainside, stopping at Tindharia, Ghaiyabari and Paglajhora on the way, to reach Kurseong sharply at eighteen minutes past ten. Piping hot breakfast would be served here.

English journalist Mark Tully, who grew up in India, has an issue with calling this a 'toy train'. Years ago, when he was a little boy, this very railway transported him back to a residential school in Darjeeling after the Christmas vacation spent with his family in their cosy Calcutta home was over. In the rumble of its carriage wheels, in the engine's whistle, one could perhaps still hear the sighs and stifled howls of forlorn boys like him. Tully writes:

> Ever since that first journey to Darjeeling I have resented the description of the DHR as a 'toy train'. It was a train which took me and many others on a deadly serious journey. It is sad that it has now been reduced to a tourist attraction and a vehicle for those who don't want to pay a bus fare, but I suppose that's progress.[2]

During Tully's boyhood days, local freeloaders would jump on to the steps of the moving carriages for a ride. He has written how they would be put off by the sight of a train full of chattering white boys. He has also written about a two-headed baby sheep in a jar of formalin displayed at a chemist's shop at Kurseong. Tully had never seen it, but he had heard a lot about it; many of his schoolmates had mentioned this peculiar exhibit while recounting the memories of those journeys later in their life. Watching the bottled, two-headed sheep must have been a ritual for these school-bound boys of yore. It must have made their exile in the cold hill station a little less unbearable, just as Nikhil Tamang's welcoming smile at Sonada did for me.

∼

Breakfast served at the railway refreshment buffet in Kurseong station used to be sumptuous. Dadu's sahib boss had ordered a large platter heaped with poached eggs, baked beans, fried bacon, sausages, etc. Dadu had bought fresh yak's milk yogurt from a Bhutia seller; he ate this mixed with the pressed rice that he had been carrying with him. Even though a pucca sahib by temperament, Dadu had the body of a Kannaujia Brahmin. He never compromised with its needs.

Fifty years later, I didn't have a chance to replenish my body or mind. The Hill Cart Road and the old Pankhabari Road meet at Kurseong. Then, as always, the tiny square across the railway station was clogged with vehicles, pedestrians and the occasional train, caught in a traffic jam! To stay out of this mess, our jeep took a bypass road above town and soon entered into dense fog. The temperature, too, had dropped by then. It seemed we had slipped into the grey, icy depths of a sea. The driver turned on the vehicle's headlights and also taped music. The shafts of yellow light melted away in the fog a few feet ahead, the music whimpered as it struggled to flow in the thick, moist air. Everything beyond the distance of a yard was a blur.

Was the driver trying to grope his way by sounding out the music, I wondered, terrified. But my fellow passengers were completely at ease. In fact, they had dozed off, resting their heads on each other's shoulders. My head felt as heavy as lead. It struck me as uncanny. It seemed as if a magical vehicle was deporting a group of humans, either dead or hypnotized, to a surreal time and space. Muffled horns were heard from time to time around invisible bends in the road, followed by yellow predatory eyes and shadows that swished past. Sometimes our driver would slow down, stick his head out of the window and speak with the shadows in an impenetrable language. I had no idea how long the journey would continue through the tunnel of fog. It was two o' clock by the watch, but the daylight had a timid predawn quality. The shrunken disc of a sun in the greyness above seemed to have been rubbed in with an eraser. Soon, a thin rain began to patter on the tarpaulin hood of the vehicle.

After what seemed to be an eternity, shadowy stands of pines began to appear against the fog, tin-roofed shanties resolved themselves under them. I saw groups of women around thin mountain springs, washing clothes and shampooing their hair. Bright flowering plants in black plastic bags stood in rows upon cottage porches. Billboards of hotels and resorts, potato chips and chocolate bars became visible; most were faded and rust-spotted, with slogans scrawled over them with green paint: WE WANT GORKHALAND.

As the vehicle slowed down near Darjeeling railway station, a young man clad in a bile-green nylon jacket hitched on to its back. He stuck his head inside and fixed his eyes directly upon me. 'You'll need a hotel, sir?' he asked me in guttural Hindi.

Nikhil had warned me about this before he got down at Sonada. I mumbled the Nepali words he had taught me, 'Daju, mo local manche ho!'

The tout cackled incredulously and replied, 'But sir, even a local person needs a place to put his head in. Come with me, it's very near. Great view, attached bath, hot water. Damn cheap, sir!'

The jeep crawled a few yards along a narrow side road and came to a halt. I peered out and saw a petrol pump, lumberyards, a coal ropeway, ironware shops and a Marwari bhojanalay. For a moment, it seemed as if I had landed by mistake in a grimy little town in North India. Evening had fallen at three-thirty in the afternoon; lamps glowed in the shops, smoke rose from heaps of garbage. A pair of ragged porters with ropes coiled around their shoulders climbed the vehicle's roof and began to unload the luggage. The man in the green jacket stood, crushed tobacco on his palm, and kept a watch on me.

'Come sa'ab, let's go,' he said. 'Give your luggage to the porter.'

I was feeling hungry and dazed. 'Let's go,' I said.

Precariously perched on a narrow hillside, Hotel Sunrise was among the rash of buildings that were coming up all over the town soon after the agitation had ended. It was still under construction, and smelt of paint and fresh pinewood. I followed the tout inside to a tiny cubicle, the reception, at the end of a narrow corridor. He exchanged words in Nepali with the manager, who looked drunk. A cheerful boy, spinning a bunch of keys on his index finger and whistling the tune of a recent Hindi film song, ushered me along another corridor to show the room. It turned out to be a tiny cabin with unpainted wooden walls; the lone window opened out to the market below. I returned to the reception to find the tout gone. The film *Baazigar* was being played on television. I wrote my name and other details in the register. A printed notice mounted on the desk proclaimed: WATER IS PRECOCIOUS. DO *NOT* WEST.

The boy fetched a bucket full of the precocious matter to the wash cubicle. Then he brought my dinner: four greasy paranthas and squash curry, the strange taste of which I have not forgotten to this day.

The cold and a hollow sensation inside the head kept me awake on my first night in Darjeeling. I heard the shuffle of footsteps on wooden floors, the muffled noise of television, and drunken prattle. The bazaar below began to open before dawn. Inscrutable voices seemed to be coming from the periphery of flimsy sleep. Then the sound of knives being whetted upon stones turned me fully awake. I got up and opened the window; it was still dark outside, some of the shops had rolled up their shutters. There was a butcher shop below the building, a naked lightbulb glowed there. I saw part of a moving human torso, draped in a navy blue apron, and a muscular arm with a rolled-up sleeve. That was all I could see. But I could hear a thin squeal that echoed like a sheet of metal being torn asunder. Then there was a hushed silence. A faint, bluish-pink light began to appear in the narrow gap between two tall buildings.

Great view! the tout had promised me. This was it.

III

SALAMANDERLAND

In Tennessee Williams' play *A Streetcar Named Desire*, the heroine takes rides on a streetcar line named Desire to come to the city centre. In New Orleans, there really was a line by that name. If a tramway in a city in the US could be named Desire, then the taxi route to the hill town of Darjeeling could very well be named Longing. To understand this, one would have to visit Chowk Bazaar on a dim, foggy afternoon. There one would see the battered Mahindra, Willys and Land Rover service jeeps waiting in front of the police outpost, below Golghar restaurant, and hear the impatient cries of drivers and their assistants:

'Silgarhi-Silgarhi-Silgarhi
Kharsang-Kharsang-Kharsang
Last turn! Last turn!'

Last turn. After this no taxi would ply on the hill roads. And Darjeeling would be completely cut off at night from the rest of the world. During my years of exile there, every time I would hear the anxious calls of these men, I would feel a sudden tug at my heart. Their litanies would blend with the muezzin's call for evening prayer rising from Butcher Bustee below and fill me with a deep longing.

One of my colleagues had an eight-year-old son who suffered from asthmatic fits. These came unannounced, and the boy had to be rushed to a lower altitude as there was no other remedy. The jeep drivers' calls would cast a shadow upon the distressed father's face.

Another colleague, who had an odd sense of humour, would respond by singing aloud a Tagore song:

'Orey ay, amay niye jabi ke re bela sesher sesh kheyay
Orey ay, diner seshe…'

'Oh come! Who'll carry me in the last ferry at day's end…
For whom the daylight has died but the lamp of the night
   has not been lit, it is he who is sitting at the pier.'

The light of the day would really die for us with the ardent cries of the last-turn drivers, the lamp of the night would not be lit, and we would plod our way to the pier … In our case, to one of the many pubs in town.

I have heard the anxious footsteps of the villagers who had come to town on work, and were hurrying to catch the last-turn service jeeps. With nightfall, not only would Darjeeling be cut off from the plains, but the settlements scattered all over the hills, too, would shrink into tiny islands in a dark ocean, the mountains would return to primaeval times. The darkness would thicken over the jeep stand, the calls would grow mystical and indistinct:

'Kalempoong-Kalempoong-Kalempoong!
Lebong-Lebong-Lebong!
Kharsang-Kharsang-Kharsang!
Last turn! Last turn!'

A perceptive ear could pick out in these slurred utterances the roots of the original Lepcha place names that the jeep-drivers unconsciously evoked. Thus, Kurseong became Kharsang, Lebong became Alebong, and Darjeeling became Dorhzeling. In the Lepcha language, each of these words has a meaning: Kharsang means 'the land of white orchids' (alternately, 'the star at dawn'), Alebong is a tongue-shaped spur, and Kalempoong is 'the ridge where we play'. In fact, many peaks, rivers, gorges and plateaus in these hills still bear Lepcha names whose sounds have been twisted in other tongues. Thus, Peshok comes from pazok, which means forest; Mirik from mir-yok, 'a place burnt by fire'; Phalut from fak-lut, 'the denuded peak'; and Senchal comes from shin-shel-lo, meaning cloud-capped hill.

That the Lepchas were the original inhabitants of the Darjeeling hills comes through loud and clear with these words. Official British documents also acknowledge this. But that shouldn't stop us from taking a critical look at the picture of a wild forested hill tract, twenty-four miles long and six miles wide, dotted here and there with a few Lepcha dwellings, that the East India Company received from the Rajah of Sikkim as a gift. Fact is, this has been one of the oldest inhabited stretches in the Himalayas and many migrating tribes and communities, herders and pastoralists, were criss-crossing it for centuries. On the part of the Company, the object of seeing, and showing, the Darjeeling hills as virgin territory was twofold: one economic, the other, cultural. For the tenancy of this hill tract, the Company had agreed to pay the Rajah an annual grant of three thousand rupees (the amount was later doubled). Lack of human habitation and, consequently, limited scope for revenue collection would have meant that the gift was rather profitable for the Rajah. And then there was the colonial mindset at work behind the notion that Darjeeling was 'discovered' by the British. This led to the fabrication of a nostalgic home town on foreign soil, upon exotic Himalayan terrain.

This fabrication progressed through the nineteenth century on a war footing; a military officer, Lt. General (then Captain) George Aylmer Lloyd was even appointed for it. In 1835, after the Company obtained the Darjeeling hills as a gift, it sent Lt. General Lloyd and Dr A. Chapman, the surgeon of the Governor General, to sojourn there and to find out whether its environment and climate were suitable for a sanatorium. They stayed there for eight months in a wattle hut that they built for themselves. Based on their report, the Darjeeling Association was formed in Calcutta with a brief to set up a town in the mountains. The years 1838–39 were a period of intense activity in Darjeeling. Jungles were cleared and plots of flattened land were distributed among members of the association. Also, and crucially important, the construction of a bridle path from the plains to Darjeeling via Punkhabari began. The Darjeeling Family Hotel was set up; a colony came up with about a dozen cottages. St Andrew's Church was built in 1843; Loreto Convent was established four years later. In the lower part of the settlement, not yet a town, dwellings for coolies and menials were coming up now as a large native labour force was sine qua non for the comfort of the sahibs and memsahibs. This led to the growth of temples and a mosque in 1851–52. The monastery in Ghoom was built in 1876, and another in Bhutia Bustee came up three years later. In 1880, the educated Bengali babus who had been flocking to the hill station as clerks and teachers established a temple of the Brahmo faith.

Thus, the tradition of people practising their different faiths in Darjeeling is as old as the town itself. But what is remarkable is that as many as nine churches and chapels were built here before the end of the nineteenth century. This was the Victorian age; British social life was drawn tight by the contrary pulls of orthodoxy and libertinism, even thousands of miles away from home. Since the Suez Canal was opened in 1869, more and more memsahibs had begun to arrive in India, but the officers posted in the mofussils did not have much opportunity to mix with them. The carefree life in the hill stations and the merry grass widows who reigned there compensated for this. Their scandalous lives in Shimla have left their marks in the writings of Kipling; those of their Darjeeling counterparts are scattered in letters, diaries and juicy anecdotes the hill people have inherited from their forefathers. There is, for example, the apocryphal story that the manager of Wilson's Hotel would ritually walk the corridors at daybreak ringing a bell so that the lodgers could return to their respective rooms before morning tea was served.

1857 was a watershed year in the history of Indian hill stations. The mutiny made it starkly clear that these mountain retreats were of crucial importance to the colonizer, not only from the point of view of health and recreation, but also of security. A few thousand feet above the heat-scorched plains, they felt safe and out of harm's way. Apart from the topography, this also had something to do with the native population. By this time, the stereotype of hill people – and they included the Lepchas of Darjeeling, the Paharis of Shimla and the Todas of Ootacamund – as the epitome of simplicity and reliability had been set.

> All who saw them would prefer their open and expressive countenances to the look of cunning, suspicion or apathy that marks the more regular features of the Hindoostanee ... They are the most good-humoured, active, curious yet simple people, that [I have] ever met with.[1]

This is one Captain Herbert, who visited Darjeeling in the 1830s to inspect its suitability as a sanatorium. John C. Lowrie, an American Presbyterian missionary, seems to echo him:

> In the manner of the Hill people there is a frank and independent bearing, which is much more pleasant than the sycophancy and servility towards superiors so common in India. They seem to be very ingenuous. They might be characterized as a simple-minded people.[2]

Coincidentally, in the year 1857, when the seeds of mistrust and iron rule were being sown in the plains of India, saplings of tea were being planted for the first time in Makaibari. In 1864, the residential St Paul's School was set up. The following year, Darjeeling got its first official cemetery and a prison; the town's population was three thousand in 1872. Eight years later, the marvel of engineering chug-chugged up the hill blowing whistles and waving banners of smoke. The dense primaeval forest cover was magically transformed into the green undulating velvets of tea gardens.

Such a whirlwind tour of history has its pitfalls: the timeline drawn to connect the points of apparently significant events eludes other events, or non-events; the eye fails to discern the gaps and ruptures in the imagined line. Our tendency to draw the line straight through clusters of happenings tends to skirt the winding tracks and dead alleys of history.

But no path in Darjeeling is straight. To know it intimately, one must step out of the broad roads and take the twisting hill tracks and steep side trails. Local people call them 'chor bato'.

∼

The young man who introduced me to the chor batos of Darjeeling was Hemraj Chhetri. His family had been living in the Himalayas for a number of generations, but his surname as well as his physiognomy bore the unmistakable mark of the North Indian warrior castes.

Hemraj's forefathers were said to have been among those Rajputs who were driven out of their homeland by the Mughals in the sixteenth century and who had taken refuge in the Hindu kingdom of Nepal. However, Hemraj didn't have any interest in such recent history; his passion lay in the Jurassic, Triassic and the Cretaceous periods. He was a research fellow in the Zoology department of our college; the object of his study was a rare species of reptile that had given evolution the slip and had managed to remain exactly as it had been 150 million years ago: the Himalayan salamander, *Tylototriton verrucosus*. These flat, greyish-pink newts were thought to have become extinct until they were found again in a pool near Darjeeling in 1964. But they are a critically endangered species that are listed in Schedule 2 of the Wild Life (Protection) Act of India, as well as in the Red List of the International Union for Conservation of Nature (IUCN).

The Himalayan salamanders live on a diet of tiny insects and aquatic plants, hibernate during winter in the clefts of stones and trees, and mate in puddles formed during the rains. There they lay eggs, and their larvae live in water until they grow lungs. Thus, natural pools and shallow waterbodies are critical for their survival.

For aeons, innumerable pools in and around the Darjeeling hills had fostered the life cycle of these living fossils. But most of these pools, locally called pokhri, were destroyed with the growth of the tea gardens. The few that were left became polluted with pesticide and detergents. With the loss of their critical habitat, the salamanders, too, were taken as lost from the face of the planet. Their renewed sighting a few decades ago sent ripples of excitement among herpetologists around the world. But that, unfortunately, didn't change their precarious existence. Just as agriculture in West Bengal is typified in the picture of a tribal girl sowing in a lush paddy field, so is the wildlife of the state embodied in the picture of a Royal Bengal tiger. A small, unsightly amphibian has no place there.

∼

Three months of ceaseless rains in Darjeeling are the cruellest, the loneliest too. Many fall prey to suicidal depression. Yet, when the town was wrapped in fog and the days were filled with a murky light, when fabulous moths swarmed at lighted windowpanes in the evenings, when the unending rains seemed to be coursing through the blood vessels, it was then that Darjeeling would work her charms on me. The desolate paths, the tourist-less Mall, the listless eyes of shopkeepers, the sleeping street dogs on the railway platform, the silhouette of an umbrella on a foggy road, the lone traffic constable, the newspaper-vendor wrapped in a cellophane burqa, the droplets of water drumming on the leaves of the tree fern, the rain-slicked mane of a solitary horse on the road around Observatory Hill, the smell of fresh arrivals at Oxford Bookshop, the amber hair of a bored belle behind the glass panes at Amigos restaurant, the scents of a lost time in Habeeb Mullick's antique shop, the rash of blue wild flowers in the crevice of a stone, the flock of tiny penguins sheathed in raincoats trooping back home from school, the murmur of a swollen spring in the pine grove on Convent Road – all these I would find irresistibly seductive.

Just as the town would fold into itself during the rainy months, the mind, too, would become at one with itself. A brooding mood that sometimes lingers in old black-and-white photographs would pervade the consciousness. Dim light filtering through fog casts no shadow, each object appears in its truest form and tone; the newborn leaf of a fern peeping through a chink in the bark trembles, hit by a big raindrop, and continues to ring in the mind's eye like a delicate tune. These languid absorptions would cast their spell on me.

This didn't happen in a day. In the beginning, I too would crave the face of the sun.

June, July and August, these wet, dripping months in Darjeeling are the loneliest, the longest too. And then, towards the end of September, the monsoon's fist loosens, a turbid whorl of light appears in the sky at noon. One day, early in the morning, tea-plucker women are seen on the green manicured slopes like swarms of grasshoppers, plucking leaves with both hands and throwing them, with a nimble, unbroken motion of their arms, into the baskets strapped to their foreheads. Another day, late in the afternoon, a flaming red sunset is visible from the open terrace of Keventers. The sudden scent of roasted corn in the air, the lacerated clouds hanging motionless over the distant mountains suggest the departure of monsoon. Then the chirping of crickets is heard one day. As their wings dry out, they emit a sharp staccato, like clockwork toys. The sun invariably appears in the morning following the night of chirping crickets: an intense sun, like liquid diamond, pouring from a pure rain-washed sky.

And then, the long-awaited morning: the Kanchenjunga resplendent across the skies, hanging like an improbable dream over the dingy, moss-spotted town. One gets up late and steps out to the balcony, toothbrush in mouth, to be greeted by the old neighbourhood morning-walker prancing back home:

'Good morning! I've seen it today!'

And then the town brushes, washes and rushes out on to the streets. One takes the chor bato to Chowrasta, turns left at the head of the stairs, and is greeted by her snowy majesty across the forest of jackets hanging from the awnings of Tibetan shops; through a gap between two tall buildings; in the porthole of the police booth; upon the begrimed windowpanes of Padma restaurant; in the cracked mirror of Lucky Saloon…

Darjeeling is not to be found in Darjeeling then because it has already been hijacked into the posters hanging on the railings of Laden La Road, sold at twenty rupees apiece, unfolded like a love letter across the narrow green ridge under a dazzling Kanchenjunga. Dadu's favourite lines are printed in a corner of the sky:

> Once again
> Do I behold these steep and lofty cliffs,
> That on a wild secluded scene impress
> Thoughts of more deep seclusion

Below it, in fine print: Lokenath Fotoprint, Hakimpara, Siliguri.

When the bleak monsoon months graded into clear autumn, Hemraj Chhetri would set out in search of salamanders in the rain-fed pokhris in the hills. Sometimes I would accompany him. We would leave the metalled road and pick out a chor bato that corkscrewed down forested hill slopes. Hemraj knew nature here like the back of his hand; formal education had given his innate wisdom a rare edge. We would scan the damp mossy stones under thick undergrowth for those veins of trickling water which would lead us below, sometimes a hundred feet or more, to where a pool had gathered. Sometimes we would only have a feeble whisper of water as our guide. It required trained ears to pick it out from the welter of sounds in the damp forest teeming with life. Sometimes particular species of plants that grow near water would betray small hidden pokhris. At other times tiny birds darting about to catch waterborne insects would give them away. The jungles around Darjeeling were like a book filled with arcane symbols. Hemraj knew how to read them.

The life cycle of the elusive salamanders has turned silently for millions of years in the water collected in moss-lined, Fallopian hollows of stones where sunlight seldom entered. Looking at the water's surface, we would find the greyish-pink creatures in suspended animation. Sometimes we would spot them from a distance on the edge of the pool, clinging to the rocks like damp leaves, but they would jump back into water in a flash at the sound of our feet.

Once we trekked down from Sonada to Margaret Hope tea garden to study the creatures in a pokhri there. It was a rather large pokhri nestled among a group of hummocks clad in green tea plants. A school of newts lived in its depths. There was a tea-pluckers' shed nearby; the leaves were weighed there and taken to the factory in tractors. The plucker women lounged in the shed after work, gossiped, and shared the food they had brought from home.

I had seen them working, immersed up to their waist in green slopes. From a distance, they had appeared like mysterious fairies, the baskets on their backs hanging like folded wings. I also knew they had magical fingers. With a practised speed that the eye failed to discern, they would pluck two leaves and a bud from a new five-leaved shoot, never touching the other three leaves that were the plants' breathers. Processed and dried, the leaves produced quality pekoe, while premium orange pekoe was made from the buds.

But, at close quarters, these women were a far cry from the fairies of the distant slopes. There were about twenty of them in the group, ranging from pubescent girls to old women. From their physical features it appeared that among them were a number of Santhals and Mundas as well as those from local hill tribes. They chattered in a kind of pidgin and exchanged giggles as they watched a Darjeeling-ko-chora and a Bangali babu meditating on the edge of the pokhri. They had hunched backs and rough skin; a few had heavy silver studs on their ears and noses. They sat on their haunches, with arms wrapped around their knees, while the salamanders were drawn to the pale green shafts of sunlight reaching into the water. The women waited with their empty baskets for the tractor to return from the factory. The salamanders remained suspended in water, as they had always been over the drift of time, for millions of years.

~

A short distance from Margaret Hope tea garden, on a shoulder of the hill, stood a church and the remains of a dozen European cottages. Here, lost amid tea plants gone wild and the tangled undergrowth, one could still find a rupture in the history of Darjeeling. This place is referred to as Hope Town in old documents. It was Hope Town, and not Kurseong, that was initially planned to be developed as the first proper station on the way to Darjeeling. The railway line was supposed to climb the hills via Hope Town to reach Darjeeling. Accordingly, land began to be distributed here from 1856; many Englishmen from Calcutta built cottages, and a church was built in 1868. But the railway never came to Hope Town; it was aligned along the higher elevation of Sonada.

A fog of despair hung over Hope Town, pierced by the whistles of distant trains that echoed among the ruins like the wails of an ogress.

~

Such forgotten nuggets of history, or non-history, are scattered all over these hills. One must turn the gaze to these false steps, these miscarriages of planning, to understand the marvellous fabrication of a nostalgia high up in the Himalayas.

Take the case of Mr Stuart, a Baptist, who had brought a group of German missionaries in 1841 to convert the heathens. They set up a mission in Tukvar and started to work among the Lepchas there. It was a failure: the climate, the natural surroundings and the torpid ways of life corroded the fervour of these missionaries. They themselves turned into heathens and were absorbed into the local society. A few of them even became planters. In the old cemeteries of Tukvar and Darjeeling, the dust that had been the ribs of these men might still tell, to listening ears, tales of the heart of darkness. Their names and years of death are engraved on stone tablets over the graves.

But history's many silences do not usually have that privilege.

The Darjeeling Himalayan Railway traverses 550 small viaducts which, in earlier times, used to have wooden boards with their serial numbers painted on them. Some of these rotted, lichen-spotted boards still stand like epitaphs on the non-existent graves of the nameless coolies who died working here. The wonderful loops, reverses and culverts on this great railway display the ingenuity of British engineers. What the eye cannot see is the fatal labour of thousands of coolies who were brought here from distant plains. What voices ring out on these bridges and viaducts when the trains run upon them?

'Darjeeling, who do you belong to?'
'I belong to the nameless coolies who came to build these bridges and never returned.'

A vital component of British colonialism in India was the reorganization of labour. As the colonial economy made inroads into the age-old feudal system, a new labour market was born and wage employment based on demand and supply was put in place. One hundred and fifty million pounds were spent for the construction of the Darjeeling Himalayan Railway – this was the single biggest investment made by the British Raj up to that time. But it really was an uphill task, in more ways than one, to recruit different types of construction workers, transport them to remote, inhospitable worksites, arrange basic facilities for them, and last, but not the least, coordinate their work considering the complex caste factors in Indian society.

The difficulty of finding labourers willing to work in the new hill station is a recurrent topic in the official reports and correspondences of the time. The worsening of relations between the British government and the Rajah of Sikkim was a problem. The hill tribes loyal to their king – like the Mechs in the upper Terai – refused to cooperate with the Company's officers. Time and money were being wasted as coolie gangs had to be sourced from lower Bengal. The despair of hotelier David Wilson, who also owned the Great Eastern Hotel in Calcutta, is evident from his letter:

> I hoped to have been able to have got the whole of my stores up the hills in fifteen days and enabled me to have said that the long talked-of Hotel was at last opened, and my anxiety and difficulties at an end; but no such good luck. The sirdar who brought the Donghars up from Calcutta tried to make his escape, and take with him the whole of these men, but succeeded only in

running away with fourteen the day after he had brought them up from Punkabaree. Had he taken all, it would have been of no consequence, as the whole of these rascals have bolted since, and I have not one left out of 150 I have got up from Calcutta.[3]

But Mr Wilson never bothered to find out why the 'rascals', who had agreed to come so far away from their home in the plains, took to their heels. This letter written by Major Garstin, an engineer, hints at the possible causes:

I shall now notice one of the causes, and a very principal one, whence the difficulty in procuring natives of the plains willing to go up arises, viz. the total want of shelter on the road and at the place itself. This will cease at the station itself, as houses are built for servants and residents in the Bazaar, but not as it affects the coolies carrying loads up ... From Titaliya to Punkhabaree is about 25 miles, and from this to Dorjeling 32 miles more, nearly all up hill. A coolie gets one rupee for taking a load of 30 seers (1 seer = .92 kg) these 57 miles, and all last rains no food was to be got on the road (at present it is procurable at two or three places, but is so dear they still carry their own provisions for the trip with them). A man therefore started with a load of 30 seers, and 10 seer of provisions for the ten days it would take him to go and return. The rains in the hill are at times incessant and the nights all the year round cold; and the poor wretches, with but little clothing to protect them from the cold, and that too never dry, without a dry spot to sleep on or anything to protect them from the inclemency of weather, often unable even to light a fire, or to cook their food, with a scarcity too of water in some parts, had their feet also attacked by the Peepsah, whose bite festers and rendered them, if not lame, at least incapable of performing their journey in the proper time, in consequence of which their provisions were expended, and hunger, added to their other sufferings, soon put an end to all their miseries; and I was told that 14 bodies were lying exposed on the road at once.[4]

British colonial writings speak in many voices. A sahib calls the coolies 'rascals', another refers to them as 'poor wretches' and tries to understand their miseries. One caned them black and blue, another made fine charcoal sketches of them; one decimated the birds and beasts of the wild by hunting them for sport, another discovered and studied new species with diligent passion; one destroyed forests for timber, another imported exotic plants for landscaping. Sometimes contrary traits were manifested in a single personality: the sahib who never missed an opportunity to shower blows and curses on his servants wrote scholarly articles about them in anthropological journals; the ardent passion that Louis Mandelli had for rare species of birds didn't stop him from killing them for preservation. This is most succinctly, and chillingly, expressed by Frederick Marshman Bailey, an officer and an explorer:

> My friendliest visitor was a shrew, which came on to my table as I was working. I grew fond of it as a companion, and yet the more I looked at it the more I felt that it might be a species which had never been seen or heard of before. As a man I wished it a long and happy life; but as an amateur naturalist I felt that the interests of science came first, so just before I left I converted my friend into a collector's specimen. It proved to be a new species and was named *Soriculus baileyi*.[5]

These traits were wired into the British imperialist project in India.

The new educated Bengali middle class that was born of this project sometimes displayed these contrary traits in their thoughts and lifestyle. The man who scripted their birth, Thomas Babington

Macaulay, had used the same pen to write the historic 'Minute on Education' and the Indian Penal Code. It was thanks to him that I went to Darjeeling to teach English literature to the young people of the hills. Macaulay had no role in the founding of the town, but it was largely because of his idea to groom a class of native intermediaries – 'a class of persons, Indian in blood and colour, but English in taste, in opinions, in morals, and in intellect' – that English literature was introduced in Indian curricula even before it was taught in British universities. It was due to him that the Scottish highlands and shaded Wessex chugged into the mental landscape of the Bengalis, and the daffodil, which he had never seen, became Dadu's most favourite flower. Had this lofty Victorian bachelor with mutton-chop sideburns not been here, there would still have been Darjeeling. But that Darjeeling would have belonged entirely to the sahibs, memsahibs and native coolies, not the Bengalis. Had the landscape of the bucolic Lake District not been inside our heads, had there been no Wordsworth and Shelley, where would we have set up our Darjeeling?

Before one visits a new place, an image of it is formed in the mind. They never match. The delicate pencil strokes of imagination are lost under the thick colours of reality. In the damp, foggy town in which I found myself, I could never recover the Darjeeling that had composed itself in my head during the months of waiting for the appointment letter. After three nights spent in the hotel above the butcher shop, I shifted to a private guest house on Zakir Hussain Road. The neighbourhood was better, the room spacious and with an attached bathroom that had occasional running water. The Mall was only a few paces away. From a window on the east, a thin slice of the snow ranges could be viewed on clear days.

I was living in a state of uninterrupted daze then. Though within the state of West Bengal, everything about the town was so different that it seemed as if I had landed in a foreign country. I couldn't understand the words my students exchanged among themselves, though the language of the West was easily discernible in their clothing and manners. It was the beginning of the 1990s, economic liberalization had begun to knock at the doors, though it was yet to make inroads into our homes in lower Bengal. But the Indo-Nepal border was a stone's throw away, goods from the so-called Asian tigers flooded the shops at Chowrasta and tourists returned home with bags full of the skins, teeth and milk of the tigers – read: umbrellas from Hong Kong, battery-powered lamps from South Korea, and toys from Singapore. The young people who came to my class were bedecked in imported accessories from head to toe – literally, from caps to nail polishes.

The students spoke Nepali, but the majority of teachers were Bengalis from the plains, working in the West Bengal Education Service and on routine transfer here. Studies had been suspended during the long agitation and the government college had become a hotbed of militant politics. But after the signing of the accord, peace was making a slow comeback on the campus. The men who had sent shivers through the spine of the state administration with guns and grenades now ran the Hill Council, wearing safari suits with Mont Blancs and Watermans clipped to the breast pockets.

One wet morning, I saw a marquee erected at Chowrasta. A group of about fifty people was standing under it with sombre faces before rows upon rows of burning lamps. It struck me as a mysterious religious ritual.

A light rain was falling and young men and women were lighting the little earthen lamps as soon as they were being snuffed out by gusts of wind. I walked towards the silent group; nobody turned to look at me. All eyes were fixed on the lamps. Cold flames danced on the pupils, some were moist. Photographs of young men hung on a large screen made of green cloth. As I stood in the middle of the deathly silence of so many people under the marquee, I could hear the crackle of burning wicks and the wind playing in the pine branches above. Another twenty-odd people lingered outside in the drizzle. Their faces, too, were turned to the screen covered with photographs. Near the dry fountain, under a black umbrella, stood two women: a mother and a daughter. The mother's face was buried in the dupatta over the daughter's shoulder. Cradling her head in her arm, the latter stood there with transfixed, surprisingly dry eyes.

It was the 27th of July, Martyrs' Day in Darjeeling. They were commemorating the twelve hundred lives lost during the two years of agitation by lighting an equal number of lamps.

'Darjeeling, who do you belong to?'
'I belong to twelve hundred lives that were shed before their time between three autumns.'

~

Another grey morning, I discovered the Indian tricolour fluttering on a number of housetops like dappled fragments of sun. It was the 15th of August. A few days later, a group of young men appeared in the college to take the university examination. They were the same men who had called for the boycott of education three years earlier. They now sported green hairbands, heavy bulging jackets, and had icy eyes. No one would have been surprised if pistols or kukris lurked inside their jackets. My seasoned colleagues cautioned me not to meddle with them. I was invigilating in a large ground-floor hall that was once a chapel. No sooner had the examination started than began to leap out from the jackets' deep pockets – no, not pistols or kukris – but books, neat fat books!

I had heard stories of the anarchic days of Naxalism in the campuses of Kolkata during the early 1970s but, frankly, I had never witnessed such a scene. This was too much for me to take, in spite of the words of wisdom from my colleagues.

If they had agreed to return to the examination system, I argued with myself, wouldn't they also yield to its rules? I asked them to stop cheating and return the books. They glowered back at me. But I kept persisting, and they smirked and jerked their shoulders in typical Yankee style. The charade continued for some time until they relented before the new, stubborn teacher and began to surrender the books. They held out the books in their right hands and touched the elbows with their left hands. It was a delightful gesture. I suddenly remembered that my neighbourhood grocer gave me my shopping, and the mistress of the guesthouse offered me tea with the same motion. Between the paradoxical gestures of Yankee-style shrugging and the tender way of giving lay an enigma that I would slowly understand over the next few years.

~

Peace had returned to Darjeeling, but the shadows of fear had not completely faded from the eyes of its people. Roads would become empty as the evening fell, heavy padlocks would hang on the gates of houses in the neighbourhood, the iron shutters of shops would roll thunderingly down. Office workers would buy English dailies that reached the town late in the afternoon and cast quick glances at a particular wall in Chowk Bazaar before they hurried back home. Any incendiary poster would first appear on that particular wall.

During my first few months in Darjeeling, I used to be peeved by this habit of the town of retreating into a shell at nightfall. I would stand listlessly in the guesthouse balcony and listen to the monotonous patter of rain upon the dark, deserted road. It would be seven in the evening by the watch; snatches of familiar television jingles would come from a nearby building. I would have nothing to do, nowhere to go. The long, empty evening would stare at me from the musty shadows in my room. I would try to recall the atmosphere in the College Street Coffee House in Calcutta at that very hour, the wreathes of blue cigarette smoke uncoiling over the tables, the buzz of voices like a wasp's nest, the tinkle of cups on saucers, the press of people at the foot of the staircase below, the pakoda-seller with his cart in front of the gate of Presidency College, and his piping call – 'Aaaaaaaay pakodiiiiii!'

'This is the legacy of the agitation.' Kiran-daju, the owner of the guesthouse who was also a primary-school teacher, told me one day. 'Before that, the bars and restaurants would remain open until ten at night. In the summer season, tourists could be seen at the Mall even at midnight. Capital Theatre used to have regular night shows. Everything changed in just two years.'

Kiran-daju's wife, whom I addressed as Bhouju, sister-in-law, added conspiratorially in a lowered voice, 'During the agitation we could tell the identity of the person by just listening to footsteps on the road. We only needed to hear the sound of boots, and we could tell whether he was a policeman, a CRPF jawan or an agitator. We had become experts, you see, experts at seeing with our ears!'

They laughed out together. In their laughter, I could hear the ringing of taut nerves.

∼

Peace had returned to Darjeeling but, just as fragments of skeletons turn up long after a natural disaster, memories of the days of terror would involuntarily flash in the minds of townspeople. The remains of burnt-up houses stood in different parts of the town.

The people of the hills have a close affinity with fire, a bond that is formed quite early in their life. The art of slash-and-burn farming was perfected over generations here. It was put to good use when the agitation peaked, when government buildings and the houses of suspected police informers were routinely burned down.

The sight of processions with flaming torches worming their way along the hill paths in the darkness of night gave nightmares to the administration. Fire was one of the two most potent and readily available weapons.

The other was the kukri. Exquisite kukris were forged in wayside smithies in Darjeeling out of the suspension springs of vintage Land Rover jeeps. The sharpness that could be achieved in the Warwickshire steel was enough to sever the head from the torso in one neat blow. In those days, the heads would sometimes turn up, wrapped in plastic bags, in garbage dumps and springs.

I grew familiar with these chronicles of horror near the end of my residence in Darjeeling. By then, the people there had gained the necessary temporal distance from the horror. I, too, had been able to win their confidence. But an early glimpse of those harrowing days was given to me by Animesh-da's father.

Animesh Mitra taught Botany in our college. His family had been living in Darjeeling for three generations. Animesh-da studied at St Paul's, when Sir David Gibbs was rector of the school. That was evident in his crisp English manners. But what had drawn me to him was his catholicity and a great sense of humour. One day he invited me to dinner.

The old single-storeyed house where Animesh-da lived with his family was below the main market, on the way to the botanical garden. Once it used to be a middle-class Bengali neighbourhood with trim villas along a shaded avenue. But I found most of the villas derelict; ugly new buildings of unplastered brick had come up around them. Most of the old properties had changed hands.

I learnt these facts from Animesh-da's father. He, too, had been born and brought up here, and had a legal practice at the Darjeeling civil court. Now pushing eighty, his body was frail, but his voice still retained its old potent timbre.

'Bombs were hurled and guns were fired in these two years. Houses, too, were burned down. But the state administration was the target of these agitators, not the Bengalis. I've not heard of any incident in which a person was attacked, or his house torched, just because he was a Bengali. I have no sympathy as such for the way they carried out the movement, but it would be unfair if we don't acknowledge this fact. But see what happened: no sooner did the situation begin to heat up than all the Bengalis sold off their properties and trooped out of the hills. Did the Biharis go? The Marwaris?'

'Your family has been living here for a long time, na?' I asked him.

'What do you mean by long time? We've been here since the beginning.'

The old man seemed a little offended, though I couldn't see his eyes in the gathering shadows of the late afternoon.

There had been a time when the sunset could be seen from a broad window, but a new two-storeyed building now blocked the view. The walls of the room were lined with fat, leather-bound law books coated with dust. He asked Animesh-da's young daughter, who had come into the room to switch on the light, to take down an old photograph from the wall. The old man cradled it in his quivering hands and beckoned me by his side on the sofa; his breath smelt like a dried leaf pressed between the pages of a book.

'Look here: late Bratindra Mohan Mitter, my father. He was the municipal commissioner of the Chinatown ward, now known as Chandmari. That was in the year 1932.'

Following his withered index finger, I spotted in the old sepia group photograph a suited Bengali babu, looking into the camera with deep self-assurance, in a crowd of white and brown sahibs posing in front of the old municipal building.

'Pinnell Sahib was the chairman that year,' Animesh-da's father continued. 'The vice chairman was a Bengali. As many as twelve among the eighteen elected commissioners were Bengalis.'

I cross-checked the facts later. His memory mostly served him right, though the number of Bengali commissioners was seven that year, not twelve. Interestingly, there were a few hillmen as well. All of them were recipients of honorary titles like Rai Bahadur and Sardar Bahadur.

I learnt many things about old Darjeeling from Animesh-da's father that evening. After dinner, I took my leave and stepped out on to the road to find thick fog drifting down the side of the hill. Voices speaking Hindi came from the new, brightly lit buildings, smoke curled up from portable ovens before the doors, a radio somewhere belted out a Bhojpuri song – a slice of Bihar in the heart of Darjeeling. The crumbling, abandoned villas stood like the empty shells of a lost time; now they harboured the town's tramps and beggars. The neoclassical patterns carved on cornices and pediments were covered with a thick layer of orange moss, the teakwood casements were rotted, the windowpanes broken. Wisps of fog were stealing in, like translucent cats, through star-shaped ruptures in the glass.

'Queen of the hills, whom do you belong to?'
'I belong to tramps, beggars and translucent cats of fog.'

I would leave behind the scenes of decay and tramp the lonely hill paths for hours. When my legs felt heavy, I would repose on wayside seats made of concrete or wood. Local people got them erected in memory of the dear departed; the names and dates of birth and death were sometimes etched on the backrests. It is believed that they give peace to their souls, that the ease of tired travellers helps them on their way to the afterlife. I don't know if there is any truth in it, but an indefinably sweet langour would always fill me as I stretched myself on a seat after an extended ramble. I would sit there and watch nature paint a slow watercolour with pine branches dipped in fog. At first a layer of wash on the eggshell-tinted sky, then a brush of delicate breeze across the rich greyness to tease out distant valleys, a scattering of cottages, terraced farmlands and the dark swell of a forest above. Now the brush would be swept up to rub in a hazy sun, bloated and pinkish, from where colour would be scraped out to lay over springs, dwellings, tea gardens...

～

This way, the long season of rains would end and the surrounding hillscape would begin to appear in clear outlines. It would also become clear why Campbell and company crossed so many mountain spurs and ridges on their way from the plains of north Bengal to select this particular spot for a hill station. From Kurseong, across a wide swathe of connected ridges, the narrow spur of Darjeeling is projected into a deep semicircular valley basin; to the north of the basin rise, as in a gallery, range upon range of the great mountains of Sikkim and Nepal. This rare geographical feature didn't fail to stir the imagination of the people who first set foot here, even that of a sunbaked military officer. 'Yet when the weather is clear and its surrounding glories stand revealed, few towns surely can compare with Darjeeling. For its situation is singularly beautiful,' writes W. Brook Northey, who commanded a Gorkha regiment.[6]

There were around sixty-five hill stations in British India though the number has always been a matter of dispute.[7] How does one define a hill station in the first place? There is no hill station in central India above four thousand feet, though the British considered six to seven thousand feet to be the ideal altitude to escape malarial mosquitoes and also to keep a station running round the year. At seven thousand feet, Darjeeling had an excellent height. It also commanded a most picturesque view. These two factors have made the town a strong contender for the title of the Queen of Hill Stations, with Kanchenjunga as her crown.

Darjeeling's great topographic beauty rests on sound aesthetic principles: the distance from the great snow-capped ranges, the deep valley floor in between, the graded symmetry of the mountains rising up to towering heights, and the harmonious angle between the viewer and the views. All these aspects conspire to create the impression of a mass of gleaming ice hanging in the skies. On a clear day, contemplating the beauty for long hours, one can see, like a cloud of breath against the surface of a mirror, the passion of the men who undertook the difficult climb one and a half centuries ago to reach this very spot and, gazing out, exclaimed, 'Good heavens! Just perfect!'

Kanchenjunga was considered the highest peak on earth in those days. The Limbus call her Sewa Lungma and, in the Tibetan tongue, she is Yang-chhen-dzo-nga, or five treasures of the great snow, so called after its five high peaks. Kabru, Kumbhakarna, Rathong, Siniolchu and Pandim, and other majestic seven- and six-thousanders are ranged on both sides across the horizon. For generations of men who live in the mountains, Kanchenjunga has remained the abode of the gods. And while the mountain has been climbed, no climber has set foot on its summit in deference to their faith.

∽

Sitting on my favourite bench at Back Mall, as the road around Observatory Hill in popularly known, gazing at the topmost part of the mountain as coils of icy vapour rose from it, my mind would turn light as a feather. The din of children from the school below would seem like sounds from another planet. Behind me, a horse carrying a tourist would clip-clop by. The squeak of its owner's rubber sandals would die the moment the men and the beast would turn the corner. Then the call of crickets would begin.

Hemraj had taught me the language of these calls. Only the male of the species calls, usually in a high-pitched tone, to attract the female and to drive off competing males. Drawn by the serenade, as the female moves closer, the call becomes low and full of pregnant pauses, to be resumed again after contented mating. But when the pitch is turned up to an ear-splitting level, it is meant as a rebuff to a rival male: 'Lay off!'

Indifferent to these rituals of love and jealousy, Kanchenjunga would pull a veil of mist over its face. I, too, would slowly plod back to Chowrasta's buzzing heart.

The season of rains would be over, autumn would have arrived, the holiday crowds would soon flood this part of the town, itself being spruced up to receive them – the signboards of shops getting new coats of paint, the horses new harnesses; the scent of roasting popcorn would suffuse the crisp air. A ruddy baby would toddle a few steps from the circumspect hands of the father into the welcoming arms of the mother; a peanut-seller boy would watch the scene with wistful eyes. Another boy, holding the reins of a roan horse, would stand in my path and say, 'Care for a ride, babuji?'

I would walk this path almost every day, and yet he would always mistake me for a tourist. The street photographers with black wide-brimmed hats would stop me and reel out in English, 'Sir, want your photo? Fine weather, nice photo! Come, sir, come!'

Sometimes I would be miffed. But, at other times, when my mind felt like a plume of snow after a brooding view of Kanchenjunga, I would tell myself, 'Let them. What are we but tourists on this planet?'

'Daju, mo local ho,' I would reply with a smile and slip into Oxford Bookstore – this notice would be hanging from its door:

BROWSERS WANTED, NO EXPERIENCE REQUIRED

~

In a tourist town, everyone is either a viewer or to be viewed. People from all over the world come to Darjeeling round the year. Before their eager eyes and alert cameras, the most ordinary details of life here turn out to be photogenic. Every individual here is a conscious actor in an endless drama, even during life's most ordinary moments. It is reflected in their dresses and manners, in the way they furnish their house fronts. Here every house, porch, courtyard, square and terrace is part of a set inside a film studio the size of a town. As one takes a seat in the toy train and looks out of the window, the tableau begins to move, the shopkeeper across the track turns his listless eyes, women sitting on stairs knitting wool flash cautious smiles, children wave energetically from a school's windows, a lone young man in a wayside bar draws away the newspaper from before his eyes to watch the blonde memsahib in the train's window, a mother shows the passing koo-chug-chug to the baby in her arms, a teenage girl shampooing her hair under a spring covers her back with an embarassed smile, a gaunt hillman smoking an antique pipe watches with silent eyes, a leathery old man watches with a newborn's eyes.

What memories are invoked in the wake of smoke and steam as the train rattles along the track it has been traversing for more than a century?

And how are the rhythms of life affected on the day the train doesn't run?

It is as if the director has barked 'Action!' from the darkness of the film studio, a hushed silence has fallen, the actors have begun to play their assigned roles, but the camera has failed to roll in upon the trolley.

~

When Darjeelingeys leave their neighbourhoods and walk up the steep winding paths that meet at the Mall, a discreet flamboyance creeps into their gait. A man bends forward a little, holding his neatly pleated umbrella like a walking stick, the jacket hanging on the other arm is folded just right; his cap is turned at a jaunty angle. A fashionable young woman cocks up her bottom sheathed in jeans, presses her cute little vanity bag under her arm, raises the sunglasses over her brow and pushes back unruly locks of hair behind her ears with little flicks of her index finger.

They walk steadily up, leaving Keventers to the left, Planters' Club to the right, then, one after the other, pass Hasty Tasty, Das Studio, Glenary's, Cottage Emporium and, when they reach the glittering windows of curio shops below the Mall, they themselves turn into animated curios on show in a town-sized emporium. Like live dolls revolving inside a glass hemisphere, round and round they promenade, chatter, greet one another and smile. Lots and lots of smiles. As Niraj Lama, a local scribe, writes:

> There are smiles and smiles every step of the mile, as it were. Smile to all you know and all you meet. And being a small town, you keep bumping into friends, relatives, colleagues and acquaintances. There are those whom you know only by sight – people you keep seeing but have never spoken to. It is normal to smile at them too. The hawkers lean out of their shops, playfully bargaining with tourists. Young porters march down the street, smiling. People stand chatting in the middle of a raging concourse, evidently happy to have met each other again – perhaps for the third time in the day.
>
> A giggly bunch of young girls wend their way through the crowd, while old men sit on a Chowrasta bench smiling in the sun. A smile is the mascot of the hills.
>
> Visitors always remark on the abundance of it, taking back photos of smiles from the remotest to the busiest corners.[8]

During one of her rare visits to Darjeeling, Indira Gandhi, too, noted the smiles and is said to have remarked, 'The people here seem to have no problem!' For a prime minister who was always greeted with sheaves of petitions whichever corner of the country she went to, these smiles must have been a rare experience. 'Don't be misled,' poet Agam Singh Giri had cautioned. 'We smile despite our lot.'

When this famous smile withers, when faces tighten like clenched fists, when the jaws turn to stone, then, Darjeeling, who do you belong to?

IV

THE LIGHTS OF JORETHANG

On leaving home for Darjeeling, I had promised Dadu that I would write to him but I never did. Frankly, I didn't know what to write. The squalid town where I arrived on a dim August afternoon had nothing in common with the quaint hill station that he had painted on my forehead like the auspicious mark of yogurt – a ritual in orthodox Hindu households when one sets out on a journey. Later, I discovered its tiny fragments in the vintage picture postcards sold at Das Studio: in the blur of a rickshaw-puller's feet under long exposure, in the chairoscuro woven on the deserted mall by leafy deodars on a sunny morning in the late nineteenth century. I sent these postcards home a few times. For detailed updates, there was the telephone. The telecom revolution had just begun in India and a string of STD-PCO booths lined the bazaar. But long-distance calls were still prohibitively costly; a three-minute conversation set one back by about eighty rupees. My communication with home was thus restricted, pared down to the bare essentials.

The autumn festival of Durga Puja was round the corner. Sales executives of various companies came to occupy the spare cot in my room at the guest house. They would usually check in around evening and depart early in the morning, after breakfast, leaving behind cigarette butts and empty shampoo sachets on the bathroom floor. One day, I returned late in the evening to find a middle-aged gentleman in a corduroy dressing gown sitting cross-legged upon the other cot, a glass of whisky in his hand and a Bengali newspaper spread before him. Seeing me, he called out cordially, 'Welcome in, Professor Saab!'

It turned out that he had already collected information about me. He took out a half-empty bottle of Signature whisky and a glass from under the cot.

'Would you?' he asked, and before I could reply, poured a generous measure.

Then he launched into a discourse on the relative merits of Shakespeare and Marlowe and, almost in the same breath, the condition of Darjeeling, its past glory and its present state of decay.

'You can't deny, sir, that this town is going to the dogs!' he said excitedly. 'When I was a student at St Paul's School here ... That was before you were born, I guess. We used to bunk Father Matthew's catechism classes to catch up with latest Saira Banu movies at Capital Theatre. Oh, what a place Darjeeling was in those days! Can you guess what it cost us to have a thick club sandwich and a mug of hot chocolate, with rich cream frothing at the rim, at Keventers? Only eighty paisa! Yessir, that was it.'

As a magical, whisky-tinted Darjeeling unfurled before my eyes, I smelt a mysterious chemical odour in the trapped air of the room. The mystery was cleared the next morning: rolls of freshly-printed vinyl banners were stacked under his cot. The gentleman offered me a business card. It read: ROMIT BANERJEE, CEO, NEW AGE INVESTMENTS. I could see the silvery roots of his dyed hair gleaming in the daylight. He dealt me a sheaf of colourful brochures and reeled out an elaborate investment plan which, if I was prudent enough to follow from that very day, would make me a millionaire in just twenty years.

I have not seen Romit Banerjee again since that morning. But in a few days, the banners of New Age Investments were fluttering everywhere in town. The Hill Council had newly been set up and funds for countless government projects were pouring in from New Delhi and Calcutta. A section of the people here were under the spell of get-rich-quick dreams. This, needless to say, had tragic consequences. But that would come later. Then, economic liberalization had released pent-up desires and the hill folk wallowed in them.

∼

It was a bright sunny morning in October. A pair of Coca-Cola salesgirls had laid out their wares under a large red parasol at the head of Convent Road. It was part of a sales-promotion exercise – they were selling the soft drink at five rupees per glass. Behind them, across a large banner, bare-chested Shah Rukh Khan was merrily taking a shower in the foamy brown liquid. The same photograph was printed on paper glasses stacked on a red plastic table. People briskly walked to the market, service jeeps whizzed past carrying commuters and schoolchildren, a boy with two LPG cylinders strapped across his back trekked up the long stairway of Bishop House. He returned shortly after delivering the load and, twiddling a five-rupee coin in his fingers, stopped before the table. He gave the poster one long stare, placed the coin on the table, picked up a glass and quaffed the drink at one go. A beatific smile broke upon the boy's face as he wiped his lips on his ragged shirtsleeve. He coiled the thick porter's rope around his neck like a scarf and walked away, singing 'Raju ban gaya gentleman'. In the film of that name, shot on location in Darjeeling, Shah Rukh Khan played the local boy Raju.

In the dingy back alleys of the bazaar, I have seen young porters eating plain rice mixed with Coca-Cola, or munching chocolate bars wrapped in chapatis. After weeks without work, they would casually spend a full day's earnings on the most expensive ice cream available at a Mall Road parlour. Perhaps a downtrodden mindset was at play here, an irrepressible urge to get into, however fleetingly, the shoes of people who treated them like dirt. Perhaps recent research on the psychology driving the spending habits of the poor, sometimes called 'poor economics', has the answer.

Even the students of our college were not immune to it. The kind of campus life some of them led and the designer dresses and accessories they sported were quite plainly beyond their means.

Second-year student Pramita Rai came to my class one day with refurbished looks – permed hair dyed flaming gold, and a black eye. I learnt later that her father had given her a sound beating for spending six hundred rupees at a neighbourhood beauty parlour. He was a class-four employee with the Darjeeling Municipality.

But such fallouts were rare. There wasn't much resistance from within against the backwash of aspirations which came in the wake of the market economy and flooded all corners of the hill society. Looking back, it doesn't appear to be much different from the middle-class Bengali society I come from, one that would soon be under the spell of the share market and shopping malls, but it did strike me as odd in those early days.

In those early days, the solitary life I led in the cold, unfamiliar town left me perpetually homesick. I yearned for the warmth of home, its familiar comforts, and sought ways to gratify it. On Kutchery Road, above the district court and the magistrate's office, there was a tin-and-cardboard shack known as Aunty's Café. A Bhutia family lived there. The usual fare of momo – a house specialty and quite famous in the area – thukpa, alu-dam and bun-anda was available there, apart from chocolates, cheese, Chinese jelly and local pickles kept in glass jars that lined the shopfront. A fat, genial, middle-aged woman, known to everyone as Aunty, ran the café with a perpetual smile on her handsome face. It was a popular haunt of the people who came to the kutchery on official work. The small sitting area inside had a narrow table and a few plastic chairs around it, but at Aunty's Café it was basudaibha kutumbakam: there, the world was one family. Men dropped in throughout the day seeking help with writing applications or filling up forms, or about approaching the right officials to get a job done. Aunty, with her untiring smile and quick mind, was always ready with advice. In a corner of the room sat an old silent woman – her mother, knitting an interminable scarf. In the morning a pair of young girls took charge; they were Aunty's daughters. The elder girl was rather pretty.

For some time, I used to have regular breakfast at Aunty's Café. What drew me here, apart from the succulent momos and the daughter's good looks, was the invisible line that seemed to separate the café from the living area.

On the way to Sandakphu, in the tiny hamlet of Chitre, a stone cottage used to sit bang on the India–Nepal border. Weary trekkers were welcome to put their feet up there by a cosy fireplace and have mugs of hot tea. The houseowner, a wizened old herdsman, would always receive them with a cordial smile and say in a slow, practised accent, 'Your country's border runs through my drawing room!'

The invisible border that ran through the tiny cottage at Kutchery Road was more dynamic. The shop at the front doubled as the household store, from where family members would regularly pick up items for domestic consumption.

The food for the household and the customers was cooked in the same tiny kitchen, while the café's sitting area became the family dining room at night, after the front door was closed. Late in the afternoon, when the black-robed lawyers sipped tea in squat steel tumblers before heading home, a corner of the table would turn into the younger girl's study. I would visit the place at different hours of the day, trying to fathom the mysterious rhythm of life that pulsed across the commercial and the domestic spaces.

∽

One aspect of life here that one could hardly overlook was that women were more hard-working than men. A number of early writings on Darjeeling have mentioned the Bhutia woman who trekked up all the way from Siliguri carrying a grand piano on her back. In fact, it was a common sight to find men lounging on the wayside, gambling in groups or stretched out dead drunk on the kerb. But the women would always be active. Even during the empty hours of gossip, their hands would be busily knitting or shelling peas. There was no real division of labour. The busiest meat shop in Chowk Bazaar was run by a woman. The butcher lady – we called her Kasai Didi – would wrap an apron over her sari and effortlessly hack the carcass of a goat along the spinal column with four deft blows of the cleaver. Women had an active role inside the home and outside; they commanded dignity and respect. Incidences of sexual harassment in public places were extremely rare. From shopkeepers to drivers of service jeeps, everyone addressed a young woman as baini, younger sister; the woman, too, reciprocated by calling them daju, elder brother. A woman on the front seat of a jeep, wedged tightly between the driver and a male passenger, would never cause a trace of embarrassment or indecency on any side.

But these were the outward features of a society. In spite of the freedom that a loosely matriarchal setup gave the women, the workload at home and outside added up to be rather heavy. This showed up in early middle age, in the prematurely coarsened skins of hands and the lines spreading like spiderwebs around the eyes and lips.

It became more starkly visible as one strayed out of the town. Lines of women carrying water or mounds of firewood were so ubiquitous that they almost failed to register upon the eye. Sometimes one saw in the distance a huge green porcupine slowly crawling up a winding hill path. As it rounded a bend, one saw a woman, deeply exhausted and drenched in sweat, carrying on her back a load of freshly picked fodder, so huge that it almost completely enveloped her. Framed photographs of tea-plucker women on green hill slopes, sleeping babies strapped to their backs, add tasteful charm to urban drawing rooms. On Doordarshan, in the two-hour afternoon slots allotted to Nepali programmes, girls from Darjeeling sing and dance with painted earthen pitchers. But the old wizened women often seen on the wayside breaking stones for road construction don't fit into that idea of the picturesque. I remember having seen such a group on a cold drizzly afternoon, sitting on their haunches under a tattered plastic awning, their faces carved out of the same brittle gneiss they were breaking. The sounds of hammering echoed on the denuded hillside like the rattle of bones.

∽

In the early 1990s, when politics in Darjeeling was changing and the new economic order was round the corner, the largest nation in the world was breaking into pieces. For a long time, the Soviet Union was the biggest importer of Darjeeling tea. Its collapse had a huge impact on the international market of tea grown on the green misty hill slopes. This was coupled with local causes: the neglect of the old gardens, lack of investments in the factories, and the agitation. Production had dropped by 70 per cent in the tea gardens of Darjeeling.

∽

In March 1995, I met a tall dark young man named Benson Kunjukunju at a seminar in Loreto College. A Syrian Christian from Alleppey, Benson taught history at North Point College. We became friends in no time because, as a Bengali and a Malayali, we had common passions: love of fish and adda. Benson had been living in Darjeeling for some time and knew the town well. He took me to the small eateries around town that served local fish dishes like tarey ko machcha and machcha ko bari, made from fresh catfish caught in nearby rivers. They tasted far better than the machcher jhol, advertised in restaurants near the railway station, painted rather than written by local signboard painters, to lure homesick

Bengali tourists. Benson also loved his drink. We began to dine together on most weekends; at Glenary's and The Park earlier in the month and, as the month wore on and our purses shrank, at New Dish near the Swiss Hotel and Penang, then a tiny eatery on Laden La Road.

The monsoon clouds were lifting and the weather was turning more pellucid every day. There was a nip in the air. After a hearty meal, we would saunter along the deserted Chowrasta late in the evening, round the Mahakal hill, and go to Back Mall that would be shrouded in darkness. There, if one looked down in the northerly direction standing at a particular spot, one could see, on clear nights, a cluster of glittering jewels in a dark valley. These were the lights of Jorethang, a small town in Sikkim by the river Rangeet. Wedged six thousand feet below in the narrow valley floor between a series of dark mountains, it was a challenging task to find the lights of the town. But somehow, in spite of having downed four or five pegs of rum, or perhaps because of it, Benson would always be spot on. The monkeys sleeping on pine trees around the Mahakal temple would be roused by his excited cry, 'I've found it! I've found it! Look, Bhatta, look – it's there! Can't you see it?'

I could only see rows of white teeth gleaming on a face perfectly blended into the surrounding darkness.

But far more difficult than spotting the lights of Jorethang was to walk steadily down Hooker Road after a few drinks. This steep hill path, named after the great nineteenth-century biologist Joseph Dalton Hooker, connected Mall Road along the ridge and Cart Road below. There was no street light and the gradient was sixty degrees in places. The jeep-owners would park their vehicles at night on the lower part of the road. After lights-spotting at Back Mall, as we would grope our way down Hooker Road in pitch darkness, we would hear whispers and giggles, and the tinkle of bangles emanating from the shadowy vehicles. Sometimes part of a dupatta or a stiletto-shod foot would dangle from a half-open door.

'Tea-garden girls!' Benson would whisper in a quivering voice as we hurriedly climbed down to Cart Road. Beads of sweat would glisten on his forehead.

Hooker could never have imagined that a path named after him could be so perversely appropriate. But perhaps he wouldn't have cared, perhaps he would have trained his sharp naturalist's eyes to study how the reproductive instinct bonds with food scarcity and seasonal migration to turn a place into the mating zone of a species.

The girls could also be seen during the busy tourist season around the seedy hotels and lodges that clustered in the lower town area. These establishments would be full of lodgers then; lungis and men's underwear would flutter like flags from windows and balconies; the din of Bengali television channels would rise from the rooms in the evenings. As the nights wore on, in the soupy, mist-laden darkness of back alleys one would suddenly come upon pairs of alert eyes in thickly painted faces ranged like Tibetan masks upon an invisible shop window.

I kept in touch with Benson for some time after I was transferred from Darjeeling and then lost contact with him. I visited the town a few years later to learn that Benson had quit and gone back to Kerala. I got his address from North Point College and wrote to him. A few weeks later he sent me an email. It was heartbreaking. Benson had contracted HIV and was living in Kottayam in his sister's house.

'Never in my life have I harmed anyone, have always loved god in my own way. Then why did he give me this punishment?' he wrote.

Later, in a long telephonic conversation, he recounted to me the circumstances in which, one torpid Wednesday afternoon in May, a momentary lapse of discretion had cast the shadow of death upon his life. The memory of that day held him in such a relentless grip that he could recall small details of it.

'Bhatta, you know gluttony is considered a sin in our religion, don't you?' asked Benson, and added with a sigh, 'Perhaps this sin drew me to even greater sin.'

I remembered how crazy he was about fish, any type of fish, and how he missed dishes made out of dried fish in Darjeeling. It was available in the market in raw form, but none of the restaurants served it. A caretaker in the staff hostel knew this weakness of Benson's. One day, the man invited him to lunch at a relative's house near Kagjhora with the promise of dried fish cooked homestyle.

The cottage at Kagjhora stood within the compound of a dilapidated European villa. It was practically a tin-and-cardboard shack with wild bushes growing around it. A group of children were playing on a patch of grass. The place was about a hundred feet above Hill Cart Road and connected by a flight of stairs. The cottage was small, but appeared to be well-appointed inside with cheap items of home decor. There was a small balcony with potted plants. It led into a narrow drawing-cum-dining room with a tiny kitchen on one side and the living room on another.

The lady of the house was a stout, jovial woman. She appeared to be on the right side of fifty. The caretaker introduced Benson to her. Two children, a boy and a girl, were doing homework on a corner of the dining table. Three teenage girls were moving about; they looked like siblings, or perhaps cousins. The girls were wearing halter tops and bright sarongs. They had the clear yellowish skin of the lady and brown, shoulder-length hair. The woman discussed something related to the children's education with the caretaker, but Benson couldn't understand her language. She spoke a broken Nepali mixed with some dialect. Lunch was served by one of the girls. It consisted of fried rice, pickled mushrooms and sukuti machcha – dried-fish curry. The fish was good, but not of the kind available in the Malabar region. After lunch they went to an adjacent room to watch television. The room was very small but tastefully decorated. There was a divan heaped with cushions and plastic flowers in a plastic vase. One of the girls brought coffee on a tray in covered porcelain cups. Then she sat on a stool, apparently to watch television, and began to give Benson sidelong glances. She had clear eyes but her cheeks were touched with rouge. The caretaker now began to grow restless and shared a joke with the girl in their dialect.

It was about him, Benson guessed. Now the girl began to run her fingers through her hair, her eyes resting on him, and languidly fidgeted with the TV remote.

'Have a good time, I'll come back later,' the caretaker said. Before Benson could reply, he slipped out of the room, closing the door behind him.

'By this time, I had understood what was about to follow,' Benson recalled. 'My heart was beating wildly.'

The girl turned her head directly at him and smiled. Then she got up and went to the window. He noticed the exposed skin of her hip between the halter top and the sarong; it had the cold pallor of a sea fish. She was looking out of the window. The children were still playing outside; their cries resonated on the panes, dark heads bobbed up over the windowsill like balls floating on waves. She drew the curtain slowly and turned to Benson.

'I tried to say something, but my throat was parched. I stood up and opened the door to find myself in a long, narrow corridor.'

A row of rooms lined it, sounds of conversation and laughter came from behind locked doors. It seemed the cottage had multiplied between facing mirrors. He had no idea it was so big. He returned to the room to find the girl sitting on the divan, watching television. The luminous screen lit up her features. He sat by her side, she turned to him, and the mist in his head cleared in the astral glow.

'I had made a mistake. She was not the daughter of the lady of the house. She was a tea-garden girl!' said Benson. I could detect a familiar quiver in his voice.

'I felt relieved. The block within me melted away.'

Benson died in 2007, nearly ten years after the virus entered his body. When I think of him now, I remember the lights of Jorethang pulsing far away in the bottom of the dark valley and his excited cry that roused the sleeping monkeys, 'I've found it! I've found it! Look, Bhatta, look – it's there! Can't you see it?'

∼

On 29 July 2008, a news item appeared in *The Telegraph* published from Kolkata. The headline read: 'Queen of Hills in HIV Grip'. A survey by the National AIDS Control Organization had unearthed a chilling fact: two out of every hundred persons in Darjeeling were HIV-affected. In fact, the town was identified among the nine most dangerous HIV hotspots in the country. According to experts, when the prevalence rate of the deadly virus in a community is above 1 per cent, it indicates a spillover from high-risk groups – like drug addicts and prostitutes – to the general population.

The news was like a volcano coming alive. But, for quite some time, flaming magma had been silently coursing up the veins in the hills, along the winding trails of the tea gardens, to erupt upon the festering underbelly of the tourist town.

V

GUIYE AND THE SCARECROWS

Like a fragment of cloud drifts into a solitary tree on a mountain spur, the spirit of a town seeps into an outsider. He buys cigarettes from a corner shop every day and forms a nodding acquaintance with the shopkeeper.

One day, as he is returning later than his usual time, the shopkeeper inquires warmly, 'Aju dhilo bhayo?'

'Aju saathi ko ghar ma party thiyo,' he manages a reply.

Soon he learns to remember the faces of all the beggars of Chowrasta. The horse boys still stop him and ask, 'Babu, care for a ride?' But they recognize him instantly, turn their caps and flash beaming smiles. He even learns the names of all the street dogs of upper Tungsung. This is important, especially if one has to return to upper Tungsung late at night. The dogs stop barking and wag their tails courteously when he calls out their names. Although he is not familiar yet with all the winding alleys and stairways of the town, he learns the distinctive smells of different localities.

The spirit of a town hangs in its air; and only a discerning person can smell it. Perhaps discerning travellers and residents can smell the spirit of a country, or even a continent.

When the P&O passenger ships neared the Bombay harbour in the old days, as the distant coastline came into view across the waters, the sunbaked civilians returning to duty after a home leave would gather on the decks, turn their nostrils in that direction and sniff the smell of India. It was said that olfactory experts could pick out, even from that distance, the scents of jasmine, coconut oil and a peculiar reek of horse dung mixed with sweat on native bodies.

Sometimes wicked veterans would vex first-timers by smearing rotten fish guts under the deck's railings and passing off the stench as the smell of India.

Even to this day, the first thing some old Englishmen do when they set foot in Darjeeling after a long time away is to smell the scent of the Queen of Hill Stations. Many a time have I seen them, venerable men and women in khaki shorts and canvas hats, step out of their vehicles near the police checkpoint below Keventers, raise their heads towards Kanchenjunga, and take a deep breath. There was a time when the scents of eau de cologne, fresh walnut cakes and smoke from burning juniper wood suffused the air here. But I could only smell fried onions, dried fish, burnt diesel, musty vapour from momo steamers, and the yeasty effluvium of raksi, chchang and other home-brewed liquor, all of these enveloped in the faint, ubiquitous odours of urine and damp moss.

On freezing winter nights, the stench of burning tyres would be added. Ragged porters would gather around bonfires in the deserted bazaar chowk; beggars, lunatics, vagabonds and street dogs would also be drawn to the circle of warmth. Sheets of ice seemed to fall from clear, starry skies and the flames would burnish the huddled faces and evoke details from Goya's dark canvases. Sometimes they would drink raksi and dance around the fire. The dances would be devoid of any grace or rhythm, but the movements would tease out some heat in the cold-benumbed limbs. From a distance, their silhouettes would appear like knots of drowning men wildly thrashing about in deep water. But the sad opera would bring smiles of joy to the faces of the wretched beggars. They would sit at a respectable distance, clap and lend their voices to the songs. The noisy chorus would commingle with the black sticky smoke from the burning rubber and enter the dark empty labyrinth of the market. Sometimes the show would go on through the night. Tourists heading to Tiger Hill to catch the sunrise might see them fleetingly through the haze of sleep, like forgettable dreams, before they nodded off again in the cosy warmth of their cars. At daybreak, the milkmen arriving from villages below the town might sometimes discover the body of a dead beggar by a heap of smouldering ashes. His mates would have left him, mistaking him to be dead drunk or sleeping, his lifeless body warmed by the embers.

Winter in Darjeeling claimed its victims from among the beggars and vagabonds. But some of them pulled through for long years. Their unique postures and litanies were like familiar landmarks in the town. Some of them could beg in four or five languages using, with uncanny instinct, the tongues of the passers-by.

In Satyajit Ray's film *Kanchenjungha*, a blind beggar accosts Anima, a married woman, in a tense moment when she is hurrying to keep a tryst with her lover.

'Help me pleeeze, poor blind beggar!' he recites in a tired voice.

A key character in *Kanchenjungha* turns out to be a local beggar boy who never speaks a word but repeatedly enters the frames of the film that revolves around the lives of an upper-middle-class Bengali family from Calcutta on the last day of their holiday in Darjeeling. The story hinges on two possibilities: that of a prospective groom proposing to the younger daughter of the family, and the snow range of Kanchenjunga coming out of the thick veil of clouds. The Kanchenjunga does show up in the end, and the young man does propose, but the girl refuses him. In the last scene, we find the beggar boy against the majestic snow range bathed in the light of the setting sun, singing a Lepcha song. The tune is also the theme music of the film.

The character of the Lepcha boy was not in the film's original script. Satyajit Ray discovered him when he came to shoot in Darjeeling. 'He symbolized Darjeeling for me because he was the only rooted character,' Ray later said.[1]

During my stay in Darjeeling, I came to learn that the boy was still alive; he lived in downtown Bhutia Bustee, or close by. Ray made the film in 1962. If the boy had been around ten years old then, he would be a middle-aged man at the time. In those days, I used to write articles and features for a Calcutta daily. If I could find the man who played the beggar boy and interview him, it would make a great newspaper story, I thought. So I set out on a quest for him in the settlements of the lower town. But nobody seemed to know his name or whereabouts, though many people had assured me that he indeed lived in the town. So I carried a snapshot of the boy in *Kanchenjungha* and cast about in the sad booze joints, gambling dens and tea shops around Dhobi Talao, Bhutia Bustee and Lower Tungsung.

As I rambled about on this mission, an exciting new map of the town began to unfold before my eyes. Like other hill stations in India, Darjeeling's demographic pyramid interlocked with its vertical topography: the upper and middle classes inhabited the upper and the working classes the lower part of the town, especially below Cart Road on the western flank of the ridge. The tariffs in hotels, and the economic status of tourists who came to stay there, also matched this stratification. In *Kanchenjungha*, Ashok, an unemployed young man, and his uncle, who is a private tutor, walk up to the Mall from the bazaar below, while the members of the upper-middle-class family stay in Windermere, the most famous and expensive hotel atop the Mall. The daily lives of well-heeled Darjeelingeys revolved around the upper and middle parts of the town, between Chowrasta and Chowk Bazaar, as most offices, banks, supermarkets, bars and restaurants were located there. The settlements of the hoi polloi spread out below along the slopes, across tea gardens, down to the valleys.

During the colonial period, the well-being of an average British family in India was taken care of by a bevy of eight to ten servants. The number could increase if there were more women and children, as was the case in hill stations. Most of the memsahibs who came to spend the summer months in Darjeeling brought along their own servants and ayahs. But local hands were also recruited. In early twentieth-century Darjeeling, their monthly pay structure was as follows:[2]

	(In rupees)
Table servant	12-16
Khansama or cook	16-30
Ayah	12-20
Masalchi (torch bearer)	4¾-8¾
Sweeper (whole time)	8-12
Bearers	12-16
Groom	10-15
Bhisti (water carrier)	1-3

Over and above them were the rickshaw-pullers, palanquin-bearers, thunderbox (wooden chamberpot) cleaners, butchers, washermen, milkmen and sundry people who worked in the bazaars, bakeries and provided other essential services. Altogether, a massive army of workers.

In the last one hundred and fifty years, the demographic pyramid of Darjeeling, mounted on the coordinates of its topography and economy, has remained largely unchanged. But there has been movement within the pyramid. After the Hill Council was set up, some groups crawled up a few notches along the chor batos, some others slipped down, felled by the contrary winds of economic liberalization. From the communists in the 1940s to Subash Ghising in the 1980s and Bimal Gurung in the early twenty-first century, everyone promised to take all the hill people to the very top. But how could the wide base of a pyramid be squeezed into its narrow apex? None of the leaders had an answer.

As I followed the paths leading away from Cart Road and rolled down through Haridas Hatta or Dhobi Talao, the trim villas and lodges fell away, pavings gave way to rough boulders and tenements would rise – shacks made out of unplaned planks, blackened with smoke and ancient moss; stale cuts of beef or pork hanging at a butcher's window, women washing clothes near filthy springs; children playing on a narrow strip of land; languid men gathered around a lighted carrom board inside a cabin; a stand of pines; a tiny kitchen garden; a thicket of plastic water pipes overhead with green squash hanging from the creepers which swarmed along the pipes; a wizened old woman sitting at a cottage door cradling a baby in her arms; a line of tiny schoolchildren climbing uphill at a leisurely pace. I would see these children at all hours of the day, lugging heavy satchels, rambling along the hill paths on a seemingly never-ending journey. On the way, they would greet the baby, pluck wild flowers and cast furtive glances at a not-so-young man who sat all day on a bench by the wayside, a blue jacket flung across his shoulders and a guitar on his lap, waiting for a life that had passed him by. He would pluck his guitar from time to time and whistle a tune:

> Who do you belong to?
> I'm sure it's not yourself
> Who do you sing love songs to?
> 'Cause you sing 'em all day long –
> But that's not your voice
> Not as far as I can tell

A nut-brown dog would sit by his side and wag its tail rhythmically.

A few hundred feet below Cart Road, as the din of the town faded, the murmur of springs could be heard. These springs were polluted by the waste of the town above, but the people who lived here had no choice. They had set up a network of pipes to draw water to their settlements. During heavy rains, when the unpaved paths were washed away, it was they who repaired them using locally available stone and wood. There was no primary school here, no health centre. High up beyond the swaying branches of pines, the town of Darjeeling gleamed like a mirage. Most able-bodied men and women in these bustees worked in the hotels and lodges there. Their underpaid labour subsidized the tourism in Darjeeling, and made it one of the most inexpensive hill stations in the country.

But it was a different story during the British times. Except for Shimla, Darjeeling had been the most upscale hill town, out of the reach of the masses. A report published in 1870 termed it 'a forbidden book' for people whose monthly income was less than five hundred rupees. Considering that a junior ICS officer, one of the so-called heaven-borns, received a salary of around four hundred rupees a month in those days, this was a big amount. A part of this trickled down to the lowest level of the town society. In those days, the wages of skilled workers and artisans in Darjeeling were much higher than they were elsewhere. Free housing, fuel and healthcare were provided in the tea gardens and a few other sectors. There was a Porters and Dandiwallahs' Act in place, with standardized rates of porterage, to protect the toiling workers. Such philanthropy often masked hard economics. For example, someone had computed that production in tea gardens could be increased by 25 to 50 per cent if hookworms could be eradicated from coolie lines.[3] But the workers benefitted from these measures and they made Darjeeling an attractive destination, drawing skilled workmen away from royal patronage in Nepal and Sikkim.

The migration continued late into the twentieth century, but it was increasingly due to the push of poverty rather than the pull of attractive wages. By then, Darjeeling had been marked out of the itinerary of most wealthy tourists. It now relied mostly on the Bengali middle class and the 'bus party' – working-class people who travelled in large groups, in chartered buses and on shoestring budgets. They often carried their own provisions and cooks, and contributed little to the local economy. In *Kanchenjungha*, the intrusion of the private tutor and his jobless nephew into the elite circle of an aristocratic family marks the beginning of changing times in the tourist culture of Darjeeling. In the opening sequence of the film, we see the lofty patriarch gazing out from the lobby of Windermere Hotel in the direction of mist-draped Kanchenjunga and remarking to a sahib, 'The most beautiful snow range in the world!'

The film's title card tells us that the sahib's name is Derrick Royals. Below this is another name: Guiye.

Was Guiye the beggar boy in the film?

~

Following the path that wound down to Lower Tungsung, around the straggly bushes of a tea garden, I came to a pool. Dozens of milk-white bedsheets, towels and pillowcases – the name of a well-known hotel embroidered on each item – were drying on clothes lines around the pool. A group of washermen was playing checkers upon a flat stone with pebbles. They stopped the game and cast curious glances as I approached them. I flashed the photograph and asked, 'Guiye, Guiye! Yo keta timi chinchau?'

As the photograph passed hands, one of the men peered at it for a moment and nodded his head. He jumped up to his feet and scampered up to a small settlement perched on the hillside. I waited, took out my camera. The white sheets fluttered in the breeze.

In about five minutes the man returned leading a boy. The boy had been eating something, bits of food were stuck around his mouth. He had the same bashful eyes, tousled hair and unkempt appearance; the resemblance to the boy in the photograph was remarkable.

'Guiye, Guiye!' the man said, pointing to the boy.

I looked up and saw a small crowd of women gathered before the settlement, their faces creased with suspicion.

This boy, too, was named Guiye. More than three decades after the film was shot, he hadn't changed a bit. Only, the Technicolor silver screen behind him was bleached to sparkling white.

～

I narrated this incident to Ms Pratibha Datta, a retired professor of English at Loreto College. Ms Datta was among the very few people in the town in whose enfeebled heart the bygone era of Darjeeling still beat. She was past ninety. When I had talked about her to one of my teachers at Calcutta University, herself an alumnus of Loreto College, she had raised her eyebrows and exclaimed, 'My god! She's still alive? Must be well over a hundred. She looked like she was ninety even in our time.'

Satyajit Ray had been a friend of the Dattas and had visited their apartment in Ajit Mansions on Chowrasta a few times. Ms Dutta would often narrate to me details about those visits, about how he had sat on a particular sofa in the drawing room, about the dishes she had cooked for him, about how he had to be warned of the low bathroom door every time he needed to go there. When I told her about my adventure in search of Guiye, the old lady exclaimed, 'Surely Manik would have loved to write a story on this incident!'

Manik, Ms Datta's husband, had been an accountant for three tea gardens in the hills. He had died a long time ago, in the 1970s. They had no children. She lived in the apartment with three cats, a domestic help, and tons of photographs and other mementos from the past. She never stepped out of the apartment, never looked out of the windows. Lack of natural light had turned her skin coarse and dry, like handmade paper, thickly dusted with freckles. I have never seen a person exist so exclusively in the past.

'The only thing I don't miss in this old age is the cold,' she would tell me. 'In the early days, winter in Darjeeling had the ferocity of a tiger.'

Once I had the opportunity to escort her on one of her rare outings. It was the month of October, the skies were a deep blue, there was bright sunshine all through the day and a cool breeze murmuring in the pines. It was the time for marinating dry fruits for Christmas plum cakes. Ms Datta possessed a vintage charcoal oven, a gift from a European tea-estate manager. She would visit the shops herself to buy fruits and wine, selecting each item with the greatest care. It occured to me much later that perhaps she was tempted by a superstition: from the beginning of October to Christmas, as the winter cold sharpened its fangs, a desire to live out the onslaught beat in her feeble heart.

On that afternoon, Ms Datta stepped out of her apartment after nearly a year and walked the fifty metres between Ajit Mansions and Keventers. It was an unforgettable experience for me. Streams of young people had turned out under a dazzling autumn sun and, amongst them, the old lady was a spirit from another era. Dressed in a purple silk sari and a beige woollen tunic with a high collar, large cat-eye sunglasses partially covering her thickly painted face, a snakeskin vanity bag hanging on her left elbow, her right hand resting on my wrist, she moved slowly like a majestic galleon. The people on the street turned their heads to look at her, the elderly shop assistants at Das Studio and Cottage Emporium came out to greet her. Ms Datta smiled at everyone as she walked down memory lane – called Commercial Row in earlier times – telling me about the buildings that had lined it half a century ago, about Lloyds Bank, Hall and Anderson, and a maple tree that stood between them, Whiteway and Laidlaw and other famous addresses that now were no more. I also learned that day the difference between raisins and sultanas, the distinguishing marks of a real cherry, and how to check the freshness of cream.

She grew tired after shopping at Keventers and said, 'Let's go to Planters' Club and stretch our legs for a while.' That was the first time I entered the famous club.

With its colonnaded veranda, cane furniture, ivy creepers, mahogany coat racks and tiger skins, bison heads and framed aquatints adorning the walls, the Planters' Club was to architecture what Pratibha Datta was to the citizenry of Darjeeling. The white sprawling building hung on an incline over the commercial ferment of Chowrasta. Spotting her, senior club members and staff came up to exchange pleasantries. A group of white girls were chatting around a table on the terrace. We sat on a sofa in the lounge. The old lady had covered literally a stone's throw distance from her apartment, but it seemed as if she had completed a journey across half the globe.

'The moment I step out on the street these days I begin to regret it,' she said between deep breaths. 'Last time it was in March. Every time I see the town changing, and changing for the worse. So many people! Where do they come from? What do they come to see here? And what a horrid dress sense they have!'

A liveried waiter brought us nimbu-pani on a brass tray. Pratibha Datta dozed off, overwhelmed by shock and nostalgia. I gazed past her crinkled neck at a pair of English girls dressed in noodle-strap tops and bandhni-printed ghagras.

They, too, had come here drawn by memories passed on from an older generation. Except for the backdrop of snow-capped ranges, everything in this town had changed. But they could still pick out the scents of those memories through a forest of unfamiliar sights and sounds. With eyes like a delicate archaeologist's brush, they blew away the dust of time and uncovered an antique door frame here, a gothic entablature there, a carved wooden gable, Hellenic faces on cast-iron railings, the trademark of a Liverpool foundry on a drain cover, the tale of a dead fountain covered in thick moss, the blur of a rickshaw-puller's legs in a daguerreotype...

> Darjeeling rickshaws were extraordinary, and needed to be. They were very smart, with good leather seats, and heavy-duty hoods for wet weather. They had very superior wheels, and a two-man push/pull bar in front and behind. They were manned by four Tibetans, who managed to carry two people up the very steep hills, and controlled their descent. The *rickshawwallahs* had a reputation for gambling, drinking and fighting. They were all controlled by a formidable Tibetan lady known to all as Annie, and their base was just below the Planters' Club.[4]

This passage is from the memoir of James Benthall, the son of an agency-house executive who had lived in Darjeeling during the Second World War. He was ten years old then. He continues:

> Darjeeling at that time was a safe place for small English children to roam. There were hazards. Among these were the storm drains. These were fearsome concrete affairs, running straight down the precipitous slopes for hundreds and hundreds, and perhaps thousands of feet, wide enough to accept a small child and foaming with water in the monsoon. It was sternly drummed into us that small children were often swept to their deaths in these, and I remember always treating them with great respect.
> We used to wander, aged eight to ten, round the bazaar on our own, or with a friend, watching gold and silver workers hammering their metals, or *kukri*-makers demonstrating their knives, etc.[5]

Is it possible to view present-day Darjeeling with the eyes of a ten-year-old boy during the final years of the Raj? What is the immutable essence of a well-known hill town that has gathered the patina of so many memories, whose every sight has been painted, photographed and written about over and over again, whose glory has spread from poems to movies, picture postcards to tour manuals? Perhaps Darjeeling is not a town, perhaps it is a narration that is being put together for more than a century now. The people who know this best are the tour operators and drivers of 'Sight Seen' jeeps. They have marked a number of imaginary points across the town – five points, seven points: Tukvar Tea Estate, Natural History Museum, Zoological Park, Himalayan Mountaineering Institute, Ganga Maiya National Park ... the narration unfolds from point to point. Armed with cameras and guidebooks, the tourists follow it unconditionally.

Except for trade or pilgrimage, travel for its own sake, or for the love of nature, has never been part of our tradition. For a devout Hindu, stepping out of his familiar surroundings always involved the risk of pollution, and crossing the kala-pani, the dark waters of the sea, was considered an outright sin. Our traditional architectural designs, too, did not open out to unrestrained nature. The people who lived close to it were called junglees and despised. Winds of change began to blow in the upper crust of Bengali society when Western education was introduced. The works of English romantic poets instilled a new passion for nature and the exotic.

For the city-bred middle classes, this new-found romanticism was offset by practical considerations. The charms of Chhotonagpur, a favourite getaway of dainty Bengali babus in the late nineteenth century, lay in its ability to revive their proverbial ill health; they built villas and garden houses there. In those days, the region was sparsely populated with tribal people who never had much use for money. Come winter, and dandified gentlemen from Calcutta would be seen walking around in village markets, asking the price of various items and exclaiming, 'Damn cheap! Damn cheap!' Local people used to call them damn-cheap babu, or dyanchi babu. Those days are long gone, but dyanchi has become an attitude that has left an indelible mark on the middle-class Bengali psyche.

If the damn-cheap babus flocked to these dry regions to the west of Bengal Presidency that included present-day Jharkhand and Odisha, Darjeeling was the exclusive preserve of desi maharajas and big zamindars. Times have changed since then. The provincializing of a pucca British hill station at the hands of the Bengali middle class is a complex and colourful narrative whose remnants can still be found in the oddest of places. In the menu board of a seedy eatery near the railway station, for example:

PURE BENGALI FOOD
AVAILABLE HERE —
BHAAT
SHUKTA
ALUBHOTEY
PASTO
MOCCHER JHOL

The curiously misspelt names of common Bengali dishes, copied by a Nepali signboard painter, read like a prayer to the god of digestion to ward off ritual pollution on foreign soil. Such menu boards are ubiquitous in all the places favoured by Bengali budget tourists. Come summer or the autumn holidays, these hotels and lodges, mostly located in the middle and lower parts of the town, would be filled with them. They would descend on Chowrasta in great human waves and transform it into any of the crowded marketplaces in Calcutta and its suburbs.

'Don't you hate so much crowd in a place like this?' I have asked some of them. The answer, invariably, has been, 'If there isn't a crowd, it seems as if something is amiss.'

Trying to understand this mindset further strengthened my realization: Darjeeling is not a town, it is a narration. A collective reading of the narration confers it a value. There is a sense of fulfilment in merging with the crowd, in watching the scenes everyone is watching, eating the food everyone is eating, joining in the fun everyone is having. Perhaps a pilgrim mentality is at work here, the idea of a sanctified space, where a collective dip in holy water grants the most private of attainments.

This is most starkly visible on top of Tiger Hill before a sunrise. On clear days, the view from here is undoubtedly a most beautiful spectacle. But no less beautiful, though a little less panoramic, is the view of the sunrise from Observatory Hill, Shrubbery Park or even from Back Mall. The same sun rises every day, 365 days a year, transforming for a few minutes the familiar, concrete-scarred skyline of our cities. We hardly care to take a look. But every day on top of Tiger Hill, in the freezing early morning cold, large crowds of tourists throng the viewing gallery with numb fingers and heavy bowels and aim their cameras and binoculars at the dark horizon. What the battery of lenses and hungry eyes wish to capture could be a star ninety-four million miles away, but it could as well be the elusive Sundarbans tiger, the bared bottom of the Princess of Monaco, or a wristy straight drive by Saurav Ganguly. When a crimson blush breaks out on the pallid snow face, followed by the ruby rim behind serrated peaks, the gallery erupts with shouts of joy and clapping. On the days the sun fails to perform its show because of the clouds, there is disappointment all around, but not dejection. This rather deepens the mystery of the unseen spectacle, a mystic longing that lingers on the faces of a pair of newly-weds. They thrust a camera into the hands of a stranger for a photograph of the two of them.

Many times have I seen the husband hand over the camera to a lone Englishman amid a crowd of Indians, and ask with an embarassed smile, 'A photograph please!' (This was before the age of selfies.)

Perhaps a key to the immutable essence of Darjeeling lay in that apparently inconsequential act. That is because Darjeeling is never to be found in its Mall and Chowrasta, in its five-points and seven-points. It is not concealed, like the pea in the princess's tale, in the snows, pine trees, hills and tea gardens. Darjeeling exists in a way of seeing, something that is wrapped around this hill town like a mantle of mists. The tourists spend money and time just to see this way of seeing. This crucial way of seeing is accomplished by placing a camera in the hands of an Englishman and seeing oneself through it.

This fabled way of seeing is composed of layers of memory that ceaselessly multiply as if they are caught between parallel mirrors. Like the kidney or the cornea, the memories, too, can be transplanted. Star Staunton writes about such a transplantation.

Ms Staunton was born in 1922 in the forest region of Assam, where her father was serving as a major in the British army. When she was five, she came to Darjeeling with her parents to spend the Christmas holidays there. One morning they rode up to Tiger Hill to watch the sunrise. The incident was so sharply etched in her memory that, even after seventy years, she could vividly recall the patterns of moonlight on the bridle path that wound up to the top of the hill. At sunrise point, there was a tower shaped like a lighthouse. A spiral staircase led to a railed balcony. There was a strange silence as all eyes were focused on the dark star-studded horizon. Dawn seemed to be fingering the skies, but pale moonlight still glinted on the deodars below. Gradually the spectral peaks became visible, light was spreading over the virgin snow, the mountains were coming alive. The wind murmured in the deodars, a halo of light began to spread at a particular spot in the sky, and then, in the midst of it, rose Mount Everest.

And then, Staunton writes:

Alas! I have culled all that from memories of books written by people who in their time have climbed that tower on Tiger Hill and been smitten by one of the most amazing spectacles the earth affords. I remember climbing the tower and coming out on top, and nothing more. Sleep must have overcome me.[6]

~

What we now see as the Himalayas were, during the Paleozoic and Mesozoic times, the ocean floor of Tethys. Then the Indian tectonic plate came floating and, around fifty million years ago, began to thrust up and fold the static Asiatic landmass into mountain ranges. The upheaval continued for millions of years, and the magma produced by enormous pressure and heat was turned into igneous and metamorphic rocks. Gneiss is a type of metamorphic rock that is found in the Darjeeling hills. Brittle and foliated, the rock breaks easily under the hammer, and millions of years of petrified waves break apart in layers, like pressed leaves. Sometimes marine fossils are found inscribed on them. If a camera is invented that is able to look through the rocks and capture 3-D images of the fossils, if such a camera is mounted on a hot-air balloon and allowed to wander over the ranges, then perhaps we would see the shadows of long-extinct oceanic creatures and plants, suspended forever in waves of rock. These creatures occasionally stir, the plants shake their branches, and we learn about an earthquake somewhere in the Himalayas.

~

Like the gneiss of Darjeeling, memories too are formed of layers of time. Rare fossils are sometimes etched upon them. The dreams of Guiye, the boy in *Kanchenjungha*, are reflected in the remembrances of ten-year-old James Benthall. After all these years, they still resonate in the patter of a goldsmith's hammer, the fiery breath of a blacksmith's bellow, the hiss of glowing kukris in a water tub, the candyman's bell, the rancid smell of yak butter, the calls of the orange-seller. A ramble around the tin-roofed labyrinths of Chowk Bazaar still yields vestiges of the marketplace from one and a half centuries ago.

It used to be called Gundri Bazaar, a large open square that was transformed on Sundays into a memsahib's sketchbook by colourfully dressed people of diverse physical features from villages around the town. In the afternoons, the din of the market could be heard a mile away like the hum of a hive swarming with bees. Apart from the hill people, there were also merchants from Punjab and Kashmir. Bearded Marwari shopkeepers sat behind brass tills, images of Lord Ganesha in tiny alcoves above their heads, solemnly leafing ledgers with moistened fingers. But most peddlers thronged the open square, sitting on their haunches, with their merchandise of fruits, eggs, grains, ironware, yak tails, brass Buddhas, old bottles, umbrellas, cotton and woollen fabric, goats and poultry. The majority of buyers were of Mongoloid origin—Bhutias, Lepchas, Tibetans, and some Nepalis. They gathered round the stalls for shopping and for fun. At one end of the square, alongside a narrow wall, a row of twenty barbers displayed their skills with scissors on the matted hair of Tibetan tradesmen; smiling Bhutia women sold fresh yogurt in square banana-leaf bowls; tea sweetened with jaggery boiled in large kettles. A blind old mendicant, his ragged assistant in tow, threaded his way through the crowd begging alms. From merchants to rickshaw-pullers, most men sported Homburgs. A Nepali ayah, her head wrapped in a colourful shawl and feet shod in silken stockings and pumps, strutted away like a memsahib. Seeing her, a pair of Lepcha women hugged each other and giggled.

These Lepcha women were sturdy and thickset. They had high cheekbones, slit eyes that were set wide apart, and thick coal-black hair. Except for the double braids on their heads, they were indistinguishable from their menfolk, who sported single braids.

In this memsahib's sketchbook of a bazaar, among the lively drawings and watercolours, a Bhutia woman would sometimes stand out like oil-on-canvas. She would have large golden earrings, necklaces of amber and agate, a thick silver girdle with hanging ornaments upon her waist, and large beads of turquoise and coral on the head set alternately on a frame. Strikingly attractive, she would also rouge her cheeks with, as Major Northey noted, 'dabs of brown paint and … pigs' blood!'[7]

~

To make sugar candy, a grain of sugar is required to be dropped in the thickening syrup; this grain is known as the seed crystal. Whenever the British in India wanted to establish a colony in the middle of nowhere, they would first set up a market there. Soon, a ganj – a small settlement – would form around the market, and a revenue-collection centre would be born. This way, the colonial economy spun its web across the subcontinent through a process of crystallization of labour and capital. A number of these ganjs are named after enterprising British officers. During the early years of the founding of Darjeeling, the Chowk Bazaar was known as Colonel Lloyd's Bazaar.

As the town of Darjeeling grew, communities from Nepal, Sikkim and Tibet flocked here seeking their fortune. The Lepchas were the original inhabitants, the Sikkimese Bhutias had migrated from Tibet in the sixteenth century. Both practised Buddhism and were registered as tribes in official censuses. The Tibetans, too, had come to settle here as a trade route ran through these parts to their forbidden land. But a large section of Darjeeling's population originated from caste-ridden Nepal: from upper-caste Brahmins and Chhetris to Damais, Kamis and Sarkis, the entire spectrum of Nepalese society was drawn by the new hill station's irresistible magnet. Like elsewhere, many of these castes had their origins in specialized professions. For example, the Damai, Kami and Sarki were tailors, blacksmiths and cobblers respectively. Then there were the Limbus, Tamangs and Gurungs, with their own languages and dialects that had been kept alive through living in isolation high up in the mountains. Like threads of many colours, these diverse castes and communities came together to weave the unique demographic fabric of Darjeeling. The colonial rulers had called it a 'Babel of tribes and nations'. On the one hand were the British and their omnivorous language, on the other were communities whose languages did not have words for village, horse, plough or money. And then there were the Lepchas, whose language has a variety of expressions for water in its different forms and motions.

When I went to work in Darjeeling in the early 1990s, years of intercultural exchange and marriage across communities had so tightly woven this wonderful human fabric that it was impossible for an outsider to tell the threads apart. But perhaps a watchful eye could still pick out the odd twist between the weft and the warp. Every day, I would gaze at the faces of my students and note the subtle variations in what are broadly termed Mongolian features. Some of them were rather tall, others were thickset. Their complexions, too, ranged from fair to pale yellow to dark. The shapes of eyes, noses and cheekbones also differed. Some had the chiselled, typically North Indian profile, while others' high cheekbones and straight black hair recalled the Amerindians. Experts could perhaps trace from this cornucopia Tibeto-Mongoloid, Tibeto-Burmese and Indo-Aryan racial origins, but my amateur curiosity was dazzled. More than a century of living together in the liberal atmosphere of a hill station and the tea gardens around it had churned up a fascinating genetic cocktail, I liked to think.

There were many intriguing faces in my class that seemed to be pages torn out of an inscrutable history book. As my mind dwelt on that history, a wisp of cloud would slip in through the open window and draw a lace curtain before the rows of silent faces turned towards me. I taught E.M. Forster's *A Passage to India* in the third year of the English honours course.

In *A Passage to India*, the English girl Adela Quested has come to British India to marry a magistrate in a small town. She wants to *understand* India. The rites of understanding a humongous country bring her in contact with a young native doctor named Aziz, a romantic widower. Together, they visit a group of mysterious caves where Adela has a traumatic experience. Did Dr Aziz try to rape her, or was it a delusion on her part? This remains a mystery, but Adela's project of understanding India falls apart and everyone is caught in the ensuing muddle. The only thing that is clear at the end is the impossibility of a relation of trust and mutual understanding across races in a colonial setting.

As I studied the novel with my students, uneasy questions slipped out of the dry academic grating and fluttered in the air. Ashen light filtered in through gathering mist and transformed the classroom into the stage for an unintended play, whose cast of characters included a Bengali from the plains and a group of young men and women from the hills. The setting was a former British hill station; the script followed a novel written by an Englishman during the colonial period. What troubled me was the problem of multiple points of view, the writer's and the readers', as I struggled to unravel the novel's structure before the class. The smell of university was still upon me and my head was full of postmodern literary theories, of Roland Barthes and the concept of the death of the author. But I had doubts about whether I, a Macaulayan Bengali babu, and many of my students, whose sense of the past lay in tea gardens once owned by the British, were reading the same novel.

Neither was I sure about whether the diverse ethnicity of my students did not cast mysterious shadows on a reading of this tale of mistrust and blind power.

~

Other than a few physical details and the amulets that some of my students wore around their necks and arms, it was impossible to distinguish their ethnic identities. Sometimes the codes of identity were preserved in rituals of birth and death, in recipes, or in the way they treated guests. But the younger generation never cared much about these things. All were devotees of Western trends in dress and music, and though not as passionate about cricket as their counterparts in the plains of West Bengal, adored the idols of Bollywood. But what was most important, all had made the Nepali language their own.

The acute scarcity of water in Darjeeling had never led to water riots, as it had in many other parts of the country, but blood was shed here for the constitutional recognition of the Nepali language. Being a Bengali, I was not ignorant of the ways in which the demand for the right to a mother tongue can lead to the demand for freedom, and that could eventually lead to the call for an independent republic. This is the story of the birth of a nation called Bangladesh. But I also knew that many ethnic groups in Darjeeling had their own languages. Nepali became the medium of communication for these groups as the majority of the population spoke it and, for over a century, was the lingua franca.

But how could a language be more precious than water? 'You'll never understand this, sir,' Newton Subba, my student, told me politely one day.

Short in stature, and stout, Newton had a shock of glossy black hair that constantly fell over his lively gimlet eyes. He was a firebrand student leader. Once during an examination, when one of the teachers was making an announcement in shoddy Hindi peppered with Bangla, Newton had stood up and urged, 'Tapai Nepali ma bhannus, sir!' The teacher didn't pay heed to him and so Newton registered his protest by tearing his answer script to pieces and storming out of the hall.

Later he came to me and repented the act. He also explained why we Bengalis would never understand their sensitiveness about a language. Bangla is the official language of a country which shares its border with the state of West Bengal. However, no one in the country would normally confuse a Bengali from West Bengal with a Bangladeshi. But the term Nepali is interchangeable for both linguistic and national identities: it could mean a Nepali-speaking Indian, it could also mean a citizen of Nepal. The inclusion of the Nepali language in the Eighth Schedule of the Indian Constitution, made after a prolonged agitation, automatically validated the citizenship rights of a few million people living in this country for generations.

Language is a crucial aspect of the complex identity of a Darjeelingey. This was addressed when the Nepali language was given official status. But something that can never be altered by wielding a pen or passing a bill in Parliament are the physical features of most people here – the shape of a nose or eyes, the colour of the skin – that set them apart wherever they go in the rest of India.

'Do you realize the problem, sir?' Newton had said. 'In Calcutta people mistake us for the Chinese, and when we go to Delhi we are treated as Tibetan refugees.'

'But isn't this also true about all the people of the Northeast?' I had asked him.

'Yes, you are right. But then they have their own states. We don't.'

Every time Newton said these words, he stifled a sigh and fell silent. His bright eyes grew dim, his jaws stiffened, his hands clasped each other like a pair of animals locked in battle.

∼

One day, Newton invited me to his house in Jalapahar. I met his great-grandmother there. The ancient woman looked out of the window at the distant mountains and recited poems and prayers in the Limbu language. When they migrated here from Nepal at the end of the nineteenth century, the entire area was covered in thick bamboo forests. Many years ago, there was a big forest fire that had continued for many days; the hill has been known as Jalapahar since then. In those days, the surrounding jungles were infested with tigers. Newton's great-grandmother had herself fought off a tiger to save a newborn calf. She rolled up her shirtsleeve to show me the scar on her arm. But it was impossible to tell from the creases left by time on the skin.

I wanted to know her age. A bashful expression fluttered in a nest of wrinkles as the lady spread out her arms like a tree. Everybody laughed. She, too, joined in and flashed her toothless gums.

She didn't know how old she was, but informed me that she was married at the age of eleven.

'Eleven or nine?' Newton asked her. There was another round of laughter.

This was a standing joke in the family, I gathered. She was nine years old when her future husband came to stay in their house. It was an ancient custom in their tribe, Newton's father explained to me. The prospective bridegroom was required to live in the bride's house as a member of the family until her mother was assured about his dependability. Only then could he take away the girl to his home after paying the bride price.

'The practice had ceased by the time my own parents were married,' Newton's father added.

When the family migrated to Darjeeling from their ancestral village in Nepal, they had brought antique copper vessels used in religious ceremonies. They had also brought their language. The copper heirlooms were displayed in a glass cabinet in the sitting room alongside other bric-a-brac. There was also an English–Limbu dictionary. Language and metal, the vestiges of uprooting.

Like the vessels, the language, too, had gathered a patina inside the old woman's brain.

The only person in the house who could converse with the grand old lady in Limbu was Newton's father. He was an advocate in the Darjeeling court. One of his brothers was a major in the Gorkha regiment. A sister had married an Australian and was settled in Adelaide. A framed photograph of the woman alongside her husband, with the Sydney Opera House in the background, stood inside the glass cabinet. No one in the house would ever speak Limbu after the matriarch's death. Another language would move a little towards inexorable death; the universe of images and sensibilities would become a little poorer.

'Why didn't you learn the language?' I asked Newton.

He gave me an amused smile and shrugged. His mother came to invite me to the dining table. I had wished to taste their traditional food, so she had prepared sel roti, a type of fried bread made with rice flour, and gundruk ko jhol, a soup made out of fermented greens. There were also other dishes. The dining hall was the hub of the house: on one side there was a sitting area around a TV set, on the other the open kitchen. Every inch of space was appointed with care and good taste; even the crockery on the shelves was aesthetically arranged. There were potted plants in the corners and an aquarium full of colourful fish. There was also a henhouse in the basement. The ceaseless chatter of the birds came diffused through the wooden floor and animated the air of the room. The wall behind the dining table was covered with posters of pop singers: Eric Clapton, Freddie Mercury, Whitney Houston, many Bob Dylans, and a few others I couldn't recognize. In this motely group, clinging to a corner of the wall, was Sathya Sai Baba, not an odd figure in the bushy-haired crowd.

Newton hadn't learnt Limbu, but he was an accomplished guitarist and singer of Western pop music. His involvement with politics and music didn't allow him much time for studies. His mother deplored this and requested me to show him the right way.

Could I, really? Would he listen to me, give up his guitar and politics, and commit to memory the history of English literature? Or did she want him to sit at his great-grandmother's feet and learn Limbu? How did I know what was the right way? If I suggested any of these, Newton would only offer me a helpless smile and a shrug.

In the late twentieth-century Darjeeling, the Newtons were more real than their great-grandparents. Years of intermarriage across caste and ethnic groups had brought forth a new generation of men and women who couldn't be slotted into narrow anthropological categories. And yet the notions that an average Bengali still nursed about hill people – that they were simple (read, brainless), emotional (read, headstrong), plain (read, easy to please), and obedient (read, never ask questions, tame as a pet animal) – smacked of the attitude of a ruler, not a neighbour. I have seen the cultivation of this attitude at different levels of the hill administration, and even in the college teachers' council. It spawned a dark harvest: anger.

Subash Ghising, and his political party, the Gorkha National Liberation Front (GNLF), used the adhesive power of this anger to bind together different hill communities into a single political entity. The term 'Gorkha' had earned recognition as the embodiment of valour from British rulers. In independent India it degenerated into 'bahadur', which means fearless, but is actually a euphemism for silent, robotic obedience. The political turmoil of the 1980s gave birth to a new form of radical Gorkha pride.

Newton's father explained this to me.

'You see, Professor Saab, I don't support Ghising and his party. But even his biggest critic cannot deny him this achievement.

If history ever remembers him, it will be because he has been able to breathe a new meaning into the term Gorkha.'

Gorkhas were the people who had migrated from Nepal. Gorkha is a district in the country and, in one version of the story, the community living there got its name from the eighth-century warrior-monk Guru Gorakhnath. According to another version, the name 'gorkha' came from 'go-rakha', the protector of cows. During the Mughal aggression in western India, it is claimed, a group of Rajputs had fled to the kingdom of Nepal; they intermarried with the local Khas and other ethnic groups and the Gorkha race was born.

I was never good at history, but I was aware of the notion, popular among the Bengalis, that the Gorkhas were people from Nepal who had driven away the indigenous Lepchas of the Darjeeling hills and settled there. Newton's father told me how a new slogan was coined during the militant movement in the eighties:

Lapche Bhote Nepali
Hami sabai Gorkhali

Lepcha, Bhutia and Nepali
We are all Gorkhas

He was a member of a lawyers' association affiliated to the All Bengal Gorkha League, the oldest political outfit in the Darjeeling hills, but that didn't stop him from acknowledging Ghising's role in bringing together everyone into a common political identity. Newton, on the other hand, was an active supporter of the Gorkha National Students' Front, the students' wing of the GNLF, but he and his friends had a secret nickname for Ghising: Mr Iskoos, Mr Squash. In public they used to refer to him, like all the others, as 'Chairman Saab'.

Subash Ghising was the almighty god of the Darjeeling hills in those days. But cracks had appeared on the divine visage, circles of corruption and nepotism were widening around him. One didn't see him much in public, but would hear him pass by – the ear-splitting hooters of his Z-plus security convoy would freeze the town's traffic at different hours of the day. It was rumoured that he used dummies for security reasons. But the silhouette of his head – fitted with the trademark Nepali topi – that could be glimpsed for a fleeting moment through his bulletproof vehicle's tinted glass, could very well have been a giant squash.

Squash is the cheapest and most common vegetable available in Darjeeling round the year. It has a bland taste and pulpy texture. Naturally, young people hate this vegetable. But the squash plant grows abundantly on hill slopes, and its edible leaves, fruits and tubers are part of the staple diet of poor hill folk.

Did the nickname 'Mr Iskoos' ever reach Ghising's ears? Perhaps he would have been happy to be in the company of Lalu Prasad Yadav, another mass leader, who famously compared himself with potatoes. Potatoes, another staple food of the poor, are an essential filling in samosas. 'Jab tak rahega samose mein aloo, tab tak rahega Bihar mein Lalu!' (As long as there will be potatoes in samosas, so long there will be Lalu in Bihar!) The popular leader loved to proclaim this in his inimitable style. Like Ghising, he too could not do much during his long tenure as chief minister, except to instil a sense of pride in the most downtrodden sections of Bihari society. For the people who are at the top of India's socio-economic pyramid, this sense of pride has little value. They can easily exchange it for the trappings of a global lifestyle. But for those who have nothing, or next to nothing, no proper roof over their heads and not enough to eat, this sense of pride is precious. As precious as boiled squash roots during rough times. It might not provide much nutrition, but nevertheless gives the feeling of a full stomach.

~

But not only squash roots, old women from villages below the town brought a variety of roots, shoots, herbs and grains into the shadowy back alleys of Darjeeling's market. They were not as exotically dressed as the women Major Northey had seen in the nineteenth century, but their grave demeanour and heavy jewellery spoke of an arcane culture. These rare herbs, mushrooms, beans that glittered like polished gems and strange thorny shoots had been collected from forests around their villages.

Hemraj took me to this bazaar on an afternoon and lectured me on the virtues of some of these mysterious bounties of nature.

'Look, this lane is the superspeciality clinic for the poor people of Darjeeling,' he declared. 'These illiterate women are its MD and FRCS doctors. They know plants that have not yet been properly taxonomied. Anyone can pull off half a dozen PhDs just by following them.'

Hemraj had a dream of organizing a seminar on ethnobotany in the college. He wanted to invite these women there for an interactive session. His dream came true, or partly true. The seminar was held, two speakers were flown in from Calcutta, but the women were not invited. Naturally. Too vulgar for the rarefied atmosphere of an academic seminar, they could at most hope to be the subject of a scholarly paper. But speakers? Nah! Who has ever heard Louis Mandelli's birds sing?

They had no place in our world but we were not unwelcome in theirs. A pretence of shopping would often draw me into the damp, dimly lit lanes at the back of the market where these women sat with their meagre wares laid out in neat bundles upon the paving stones. By then, the real Darjeeling had completely effaced the imaginary town that Dadu had sketched in my mind. I would catch its fleeting shadows in the vintage photographs displayed in Das Studio and on the shelves of Oxford Bookstore. I would also find them in the attire of these old women, in their solemn postures, in the frantic calls of orange-sellers, and in the gestures of tea-seller women who teased out the fragrance of leaves by briskly rubbing them and holding out their cupped palms under the discerning nostrils of customers.

The vibrant life of old Chowk Bazaar was to be found in the sketches and watercolours made by amateur artists of the Raj. Their crude imitations hung in souvenir shops around Chowrasta: colourful ethnic stereotypes painted on pieces of black cloth. Most of these figures were the offshoots of colonial anthropology, passed through the hands of generations of copyists. But they appealed to the tastes of average tourists who would ritually visit the tea gardens and have their photographs taken as they mimicked these stereotypes. They would pose before lensmen dressed in hired costumes and jewellery, the men sporting kukris and the women carrying tea baskets.

And yet, perhaps those old colonial artworks had an element of truth: an anxiety to hold on to the ineluctable passage of time. An anxiety that goaded the watercolourists to capture the translucent shadow of a cloud on rippling waters, the minute details of the hunched figures, the creased faces, the pyramids of fruits, and other scenes that had unfolded here upon the bazaar chowk one and a half centuries ago, under the delicate light of an autumn afternoon. After all these years, the lines and tones still called up confused emotions, so flimsy that they crumbled before the memory could seize them. Sometimes a certain mood hung like a lingering fragrance in the labyrinthine alleys of the bazaar, amid the shuffle of feet and the low chatter of the women selling herbs. The mood persisted, but the images that had evoked it had been lost forever, the way the shadow of a cloud is lost upon water, a rainbow is lost upon a cloud, the way empires were lost in the subcontinent.

～

I woke up late one day and went to the market to find the lanes empty, the shops closed, and dogs sleeping upon heaps of uncollected garbage. It seemed the life of the market had been suspended by some magic.

There was a bandh in town.

Earlier in the morning, the dead body of a municipal councillor had been found in Chowk Bazaar. The killers had slit his jugular and hung him on an old gas-lamp post, a relic from British times. Hushed voices swirled about behind closed doors. Rumour was rife that the councillor had been seen the night before drinking with his two assassins at a bar on Nehru Road. After the booze, the three were seen walking to the market clasping one another's shoulders like old buddies; one of them was whistling a tune. The councillor was tottering, it was said, but whether due to the effects of drink or terror couldn't be verified. Some even suggested that the killers had knifed him inside the bar and were carrying the lifeless body upright, as if walking him along the streets. It had left a trail of blood upon the flagstones of Chowk Bazaar, but the dogs had licked it off before the police arrived.

It was a Wednesday.

~

All political uprisings in the Darjeeling hills have made use of two weapons: bandh and fire. Both have a suddenness and unpredictability, a whiplash impact upon the senses, both send a crackle of panic racing along the nervous system. A fire in Darjeeling in the darkness of night can be seen from afar. The flames leap into the skies and light up the hillside; the sparks, following the whims of the wind, fly and set aflame the dry bushes and makeshift tenements below, and spread in different directions. A fire brings out the topographic reality of a hill town with terrifying urgency.

So does a bandh. It shows how dependent the life of a hill town is on the plains. A road blockade cuts off essential supplies and effectively chokes its beating heart. The familiar din of traffic is turned off and an uneasy silence descends. One can hear the murmur of a forgotten spring and the call of cicadas. Sunlight weaves unrecognizable patterns on the deserted market square.

But no less tense than the bandh is the anticipation of it, the preparation for an indefinite strike.

It would generally begin in the morning with a new poster on a particular stretch of the wall at Chowk Bazaar, a poster hastily scrawled with black and red ink on old newspaper. Soon a small crowd of shopkeepers, passers-by and porters would gather in front of it. The gentlefolk would slow down on their way to work and cast furtive glances. The two local dailies, *Sunchari* and *Aaja Bholi*, would fly off the news stands in no time. Within a couple of hours, the news would spread far and wide, like a forest fire. By early afternoon, long queues would form before cash counters at the banks – ATMs were then still a few years away. The crowd in front of the Chowk Bazaar wall would remain, though its composition would change from time to time. The permanent ones were invariably the illiterate porters and labourers. They would try to assess the depth of fury expressed in the words by studying the stubborn curves and slashes of the script. Perhaps a procession might begin at the railway station and proceed to the district magistrate's office.

By late afternoon, paramilitary vehicles would roll into the streets. Long lines of water cans would appear at the Lal Diki spring, water carts would trundle away in different directions. Porters laden with baskets of provisions would walk briskly, followed by well-to-do citizens of the town. Their hard-up counterparts would arrive late at the market, after the pumped up prices at the greengrocer's would have subsided, when the fruit-sellers would scramble to sell off their goods before the end of the day. Then the last-turn jeeps would leave for Sukhiapokhri and Lebong, their rooftop carriers loaded with sacks of potatoes and egg trays. Daylight would die as lead-coloured clouds stole up on the brow of the hills. The iron shutters of the shops would roll down thunderingly like curtains over a suspense-filled play. The old bearded Muslim baker would toss the last unsold loaf to the ragged madman before putting the fire in the oven to sleep. Clutching the loaf to his breast like a trophy, the merry madman would look around to share his ecstasy but not a soul would be seen in the market square. Chowk Bazaar would have the look of a ghost town.

In Darjeeling, a bandh was not an event, it was a state of mind. Bandhs lurked in the corners of the eyes of its citizens, in their hurried gait. Normal life here meant the interlude between two bandhs, like in a city caught in war. Here, on a bright sunny day, one would see jars of pickles and trays of chopped vegetables laid out on the roofs – readiness for a future bandh. I have heard that many well-to-do homes had facilities to store a month's requirement of water and three months' supply of provisions. During the World Wars, houses in Europe had bunkers dug under them. The gentlefolk of Darjeeling carried such bunkers with them, like hermit crabs, and slipped in at the whiff of danger. Whenever trouble would break out on campus, I would see on many of these faces eyes that seemed to be peering through vent holes.

> I am an unemployed,
> thirty eight year old 'youth' in Darjeeling
> (name withheld, naturally).
> My education cut short
> all thanks to the agitation of 1986.
> It's as if the last 22 years
> has been going around on its own axis.
> I roam the streets of my hometown
> and try to act as nonchalant as could be;
> like when we were teenagers.

This is from a poem by Yumita Rai, about a saiduwa chora, a black sheep, who lives off his father's meagre pension. He is lodged at the Eden Hospital with a jaundiced liver, where nobody comes to visit him except his tired mother. In this he is better than his neighbour in the next bed, a young man like him, slowly dying, whom nobody comes to visit. He is, they are, the lost generation: frustrated foot-soldiers of a failed revolution turned alcoholics and drug addicts. Their dreams have rotted away, their memories are scarred. They are now scarecrows, and behave as the wind behaves.

VI

PEMBA'S UMBRELLA

Off Cart Road, a few paces from the market square, a lane zigzags down through a shady pine grove to a neighbourhood named Haridas Hatta. In the 1990s, this was a quiet neighbourhood of mostly middle-class office workers. I had shifted from the guesthouse on Zakir Hussain Road to a small rented apartment here. From my tiny balcony, the botanical garden and part of the jail compound could be seen a few hundred feet below on the hillside. To the right, a swathe of Happy Valley tea garden rolled down like a green glacier. The convicts played volleyball in the afternoons on a bald patch of ground inside the prison walls. The thud of the ball would reach up to me half a second after the Lilliputian players had hit it. The life of the prisoners seemed forever suspended in this half-second. I could also hear, at different hours of the day and coming from different directions, the tinkling of temple bells and the deep sounds of church bells, the muezzin's call, and the booming horns from monasteries. In the dead of the night, the whistles of the toy trains' engines would wail like banshees. I have never been able to figure out why they blew them at such odd hours; perhaps the gangmen in the loco-shed fired the boilers to fend off the freezing cold.

On the whole, Haridas Hatta was a good place to stay. The water scarcity was not so acute here because of a trickling spring. But the street dogs made my late-night returns difficult. They were bigger and fiercer than their counterparts on Zakir Hussain Road, and some had marks of pedigree on them. They slept through the day and took over the mohalla at nightfall. Here, too, I was compelled to learn their names. They also learnt my scent. I cannot say who did what first, but everywhere the birth of chumminess with local street dogs is the surest proof of the conversion of an outsider into a proper resident of the neighbourhood.

Now I would walk back to my flat at any hour of the night, calling out names like Jimmy, Bhalu and Tiger, digging tunnels of acquiescent silence through an impenetrable wall of barking. Their noisy vigil would continue through the night, especially on moonlit nights. The chorus of dogs would fan out across the dark tea garden and elicit an ululating response from their wild canine cousins, the jackals.

Jackals were brought to Darjeeling as scavengers at the end of the nineteenth century by the Maharajah of Burdwan, who owned extensive properties in town which he rented out to Europeans. These animals have been here since then. But growing urbanization had pushed them to the town's forested fringes, especially the shrub-covered ditches around the tea gardens. At dusk, Happy Valley would reverberate with their chorus, and a nostalgia for the plains of Bengal, its emerald paddy fields and steaming marshes would unfold through layers of mist. If there is anything in Darjeeling that the Bengalis can truly claim as their contribution, it is these jackals.

But the street dogs here never mated with the jackals. These animals, their thick fur infested with fleas and marked by the scars of old fights, displayed an interesting genetic mixture. They were like living museums of the town's colonial past. During the Raj days, the memsahibs and babalogs who flocked to Darjeeling to escape the dreaded Indian summer usually stayed in rented lodges and guest houses. They brought with them their retinue of servants, pet animals and even potted plants. Through the long months of summer, passions swirled at endless fancy-dress balls, fêtes and amateur theatricals in clubs and the cantonment. In this assembly of grass widows and unattached officers on leave, such passions often bordered on the illicit, and were sometimes passed on to their canine pets who must have sought quick fulfilment behind rose bushes and around garden fences. The streets of contemporary Darjeeling teemed with these touch-and-go romances of the past, written in the shape of a snout or the shade of a coat, where Saint Bernard, Golden Retriever and local Bhutia strains had commingled.

∼

Late at night, when Haridas Hatta became the kingdom of dogs, I would plod my way back to my apartment. By then, the town would have passed on a strange ennui into my bones. Other than the few hours I devoted to teaching, the greater part of my day would be spent in aimless wanderings, browsing at Oxford Bookstore, endless adda at the teachers' mess, and boozing with Benson – at Penang, the Orient and, when our purses thinned, at the flyblown joints behind the stables.

My professional identity in this small town, where everybody seemed to know one another, never cut into my freedom. The tolerance and breadth of mind of the ordinary people of Darjeeling, I found many times, was greater than the Kanchenjunga. But my senior Bengali colleagues grew anxious and missed no opportunity to counsel me. Most of them pined for a transfer to Calcutta. They read stale Bengali dailies that reached the town by late afternoon mail and shopped, with scrupulous care, for the stale fish that came from the plains. Some of them slipped on balaclavas if they needed to step out after dark. The spirit of Darjeeling never found a way to infect them.

Sometimes, I would give ear to their words of wisdom and pull out old notebooks from under the chaos of books and magazines on my desk. The doctoral research I was doing in Calcutta, which I had abandoned midway after I came here, struck me as impenetrable, the work of a stranger. I could not recognize the self that had sloughed off me. Leaving the notebooks open, I would step out of my desolate apartment and saunter up to the Mall. I would sit on an empty bench and watch the spectacle of life unfold as in a kaleidoscope: a dhoti-clad babumoshai with a Duaflex camera hanging on his chest; a breathless woman with a beanbag bottom walking up the steep road; a listless child with pink candyfloss in its hand; blue varicose veins twitching upon the thighs of an old memsahib below her khaki shorts. Sometimes, I would let my eyes be mesmerized by limpid forms and colour. At other times, I would let them pick out an interesting scene from the welter of moving images.

A young woman on a horse posing before the camera, for instance.

The woman, newly married, with mehndi-painted hands and long hair braided in the traditional style, was dressed in ill-fitting jeans that probably belonged to her husband. She was perched on a young white unsaddled horse. While the cameraman with his trademark black hat took aim, the husband, standing beside him, directed her. But the lady appeared to be fighting some strange discomfiture. The horse's back that she pressed with her thighs rippled unstoppably and an embarassed reddening spread over her face. The husband was too absorbed with the composition of the photograph to notice it, but it didn't escape the experienced eyes of the photographer. He fidgeted with the lenses and waited for the horse to stand still, for the woman to have her fill of that queer, indecent sensation. In the bustle of the crowded Mall, I, together with the photographer and perhaps the horse, became witness to the most secret experience of an unknown woman.

I would return to Haridas Hatta carrying the images I had raked up during the day. Mouldy air would greet me as I opened the door to my apartment, my eyes would take a few seconds to adjust to the dimness of a late murky afternoon. I would switch on the light and a swarm of cockroaches would scuttle away from the half-eaten slice of bread I had left at breakfast.

One of the walls of my bedroom was actually a side of the hill; tiny beads of water appeared on it during the monsoon months. I could feel the mountain exhale its moist breath. I had covered the damp splotches with old photographs of Darjeeling – Dadu's nostalgia mounted on laminated cardboard. My clothing would lie heaped in a corner, books and cassettes would be strewn on the unmade bed, the blanket tangled up to resemble the figure of a sleeping man. A lone sock hanging upon the bedstead mimicked the whiskered creature in Dali's *The Persistence of Memory*. Time was melting away.

After a dreamless sleep, my eyes opened on a vintage photograph of the town, probably taken from the top of Observatory Hill.

It was a bright sunny day in 1903, the serrated line of snow stretched across the sky. Down below, in the foreground, a scatter of gingerbread cottages lined with tall pines could be seen. But there was not a soul in sight; the sun and the trees had woven a neat chairoscuro on the winding hill path.

Where had the townspeople gone? Familiar lines came hopelessly to my lips:

And, little town, thy streets for evermore
Will silent be; and not a soul to tell
Why thou art desolate, can e'er return

Light filtering in through grimy windowpanes moved over the photograph, the chiaroscuro changed. The patter of rain stopped; a chorus of crickets began in the pine grove; a lone birdcall scratched the surface of silence and ceased. Feeling too listless to begin the morning rites, I gazed at the lighted windowpanes and tried to guess the hour. Suddenly, with a shock, I realized it was late afternoon. I had returned after a ramble and fallen asleep. Daylight was fading. Lying still on the bed, I pricked up my ears to hear the cocks crow in the coolie lines below the tea garden, homebound cows moo, a dog bark, a baby wail and a woman babble to pacify it, a man's voice call out a name, 'Maiiiili!' and the reply, in a young girl's voice, come from afar, 'Hajoooor!'

Were these sounds there on that sunny day in 1903? Perhaps they were, etched on time for all these years like images on a Grecian urn. The rains had uncovered the fossil sounds from the earth.

∼

From the Kutchery, a chor bato went up across the old graveyard to the college premises. I used it so frequently, at different hours of the day, that even after all these years I just need to close my eyes to recall all the details along the way. The path came alive in the morning with the lively chatter of children going to schools. Then it remained desolate for a few hours. The silent air of the graveyard was ruffled occasionally by the noise of automobiles on Cart Road. Young men and women, many of them students of the college, arrived in pairs and found secluded nooks behind the mossy gravestones. On bright afternoons, when sunlight fell on grass across the old pines and magnolias, women from the tenements below came here to chat and knit wool. Their children flew kites and chased butterflies. As the day waned, the place became the haunt of drug addicts.

But the true spirit of the place loomed up on grey, foggy days. I saw a large Himalayan eagle here, perched on a cenotaph, on such a day. It was a full-grown bird. With folded wings raised up and head turned sideways, it struck such an arresting pose that, for a moment, I thought it was part of the stonework. Its plumes had the tone of rain-washed basalt and its eyes were like drops of molten sulphur. The bird was giving me a piercing look.

After a brief shower in the afternoon, the chor bato would usually be deserted. A weak sun would peep through orchid-covered branches; a pair of squirrels would play with pine cones; a tit-babbler would hop about on the sunlit grass in search of worms.

Three Bhutia girls hurrying down the path with baskets strapped across their heads would be startled to find me standing there and vanish behind the bushes. Their titter would float in the still air like a windblown leaf and stick to my consciousness.

There are hundreds of decrepit burial grounds in former British civil stations all over this subcontinent. Many of them are lost forever, eaten away by a river or taken over by real estate. In big cities, the homeless have pitched their hovels there. They live in lean-tos against neo-Gothic mausoleums. They sleep, dream, make love, cook food, grind spices upon the gravestones, hang clotheslines across them. The marble angels and fairies have been wrenched away to adorn private gardens, the tablets have gone to paan stalls – the chill of death retained in ancient marble keeps betel leaves fresh and cool. In the abandoned graveyards, under six feet of earth, the bones of the dead slowly turn to dust and mix, depending on location, with fine alluvium or grainy laterite. Up in the Himalayas, the shape of a Germanic skeleton is sometimes superimposed upon the marine fossils of the Tethys.

∽

One drizzly morning, as I was hurrying down the shortcut to buy cigarettes, I saw a tall white girl standing alone in the cemetery in front of a fenced, postbox-shaped memorial. She wore a plain khadi kurta-pajama and a mauve stole around her shoulders. Her wet blonde hair was pressed against the back of her head and neck. I couldn't gather her age as her face was turned towards the cenotaph, but from her dress she appeared to belong to that tribe of European backpackers who usually come to Darjeeling en route from Benares to Kathmandu. Here, she was probably standing before the grave of a great-granduncle, a forgotten civilian who had died here a century ago of loneliness and a rotten liver, at an age younger than she was.

There are many such stories in the old graveyard in Darjeeling, and many such visitors. They look around patiently for names that come up ritually at Easter, Christmas and other family gatherings. Finding them etched upon moss-covered gravestones, unexpected bonds are formed with this far-off Indian hill station that once belonged to them. Darjeeling continually mellows and rediscovers itself with these new-found bonds.

But I couldn't find any trace of the girl on my way back, not even a stalk of a flower on the grave in front of which she was standing. Perhaps it has already reached a girl in Mount Hermon or St Robert's School via her classmate, I thought. The homage paid to a nineteenth-century Englishman had probably been co-opted to express the passion of a schoolboy. But the name written on stone was not that of an Englishman. It was that of Alexander Csoma de Kőrös, who died in 1842. I had heard the name before, but couldn't remember where.

The following day, there was a seminar of the English Study Circle at Loreto College. Though I found these programmes insipid and tiresome, I couldn't resist the lure of the thick cheese sandwiches and brownies that Mother Damien, the principal of the college, served. Anaemic Eng-lit ladies would present abstruse papers on the suppressed libido of D.H. Lawrence's women even as monkeys masturbated on the rhododendron trees in the garden outside. I would slouch in a corner, watching them, and wait for the coffee break.

That day, after the seminar, Mother introduced me to the girl I had seen in the graveyard. Her name was Julia Griffith. In her early thirties, Julia had come from England to research the Lepcha tribe settled in Darjeeling. I met her again that evening at a tea party in Pratibha Datta's apartment. When I mentioned where I had seen her the day before, Julia said, 'Oh really? I was there to see the grave of Csoma de Kőrös.'

I confessed that I knew nothing about him, and this gave her an opportunity to launch into an excited talk on the life and work of this great man.

I have forgotten what exactly she said that evening, but I remember how the irises of her eyes changed colour from frosted grey to limpid green as she talked.

~

Csoma de Kőrös, a Hungarian, came to India in search of the ancestors of his race in central Asia. He made long preparations for this trip, learnt many languages and studied a great deal about Oriental religions. He set out in the year 1820, when he was thirty-six, and his plan was to travel on foot along the entire length of the Silk Route. It was a difficult journey – he passed through some of the most remote, dangerous lands, ravaged by war and plague, and, on reaching India, he worked briefly as a spy for the East India Company. But his destination was Mongolia, and he planned to go there via Tibet. Csoma spent five years in a remote gompa in Leh, studying the Tibetan language and literature. But one thing or another held him back and the journey was repeatedly deferred. He became the librarian at the Asiatic Society in Calcutta, wrote books, and then, in 1842, set out for Darjeeling on his way to Tibet. He was fifty-eight at the time, ready to undertake the last leg of a great journey that had started twenty-three years earlier and a thousand miles away. Csoma reached Darjeeling in the sunny month of April and waited there for the necessary permission from the Rajah of Sikkim to pass through his territory. It came, but too late. The death valley of the Terai had already injected the fatal malarial parasite into his bloodstream.

There is a strong romantic element in Kőrös's life story, and that seemed to have attracted Julia. A fascination for the exotic, for a world that is light years away from one's own, had brought an English girl to Darjeeling to study the Lepchas and their lost ways of life. She was staying in the Chalet Hotel in Chowrasta and was spending her days visiting libraries and settlements around town. After we met at Ms Datta's house, I began to occasionally accompany her.

Julia had a few things in common with Adela of *A Passage to India*. Like the woman in the novel, she too wanted to understand India through the prism of Western rationalism. She took down the details of Lepcha rituals and faith in a blue Stamford notebook with the cold curiosity of a naturalist, but she had a sound professionalism that Adela lacked. In fact, she knew much more about different aspects of tribal life in India than I did. She had travelled to more places in the three months that she had been here than I could have imagined travelling to in thirty years.

One day, Julia said to me, 'You see, after his return from South Africa, Gandhi came to know this vast country by travelling in the railways. Most of his writings, too, were in English. The man who played such a big role in driving away the British from India was using two key elements of the Empire, railways and the English language. Isn't that marvellous?'

I told her about my childhood, about how strong anti-British sentiments were more than two decades after Independence. When I was a little boy, I used to watch patriotic movies with my parents, movies on the lives of Bengal revolutionaries like Bagha Jatin, Khudiram Bose and Netaji Subhas. In these films, the scenes were interspersed with jerky newsreels of pre-Independence times, of processionists carrying national flags and chanting Vande Mataram, of policemen in white uniforms and pith helmets beating them up mercilessly. The brutal English officers, played by local actors wearing wigs and layers of white paint, spoke a Sanskritized Bengali in a funny accent. Popular patriotic songs were played in chorus in the background. On screen, the image of Mother India faded in over the map of India from time to time. The woman who played it was a familiar model from Horlicks advertisements. The films were in black and white, and the blood that gushed out of the wounds of dying revolutionaries was a thick velvety black. Sitting in the dark auditorium, watching the scenes over the silhouettes of heads, I could feel the black blood boiling in my veins. Dadu would cool it down with doses of Wordsworth and phrasal verbs when I got back home.

The story of my grandfather brought a smile to Julia's face.

'I can understand,' she said. 'Perhaps there still are men like him. The Bengali babus were the butt of jokes, but there was also sympathy and respect on both sides. After the transfer of power, when the officers were leaving this land forever, lots of sad emotions were displayed.'

Julia always called our country's Independence the transfer of power. But there was not a trace of cynicism in this. She and I saw the event of 1947 from two different perspectives, just as the people of India and Nepal see the Kanchenjunga massif – the same snow-capped ranges, but slightly different in outline.

'Yes, I have heard about it,' I said. 'Those very men who had once shouted slogans like "Go Back!" and "Quit India!", embraced the departing Englishmen and gave them flowers. In countless railway stations, scenes of melancholy farewell were played out while sad whistles and the sighs of engines echoed in the background.'

'Look, Britain needed India just as India needed Britain. The nostalgia for the Raj is still alive in my country, among the older generation. But more than that, there is also a feeling of gratitude. Without India, we could never have many good things in our system. India was a laboratory of public governance.'

Julia would talk as she walked, stop to view something, and change the topic. Meanwhile, the mist would lift and the tea gardens below would come into view: waves of rain-washed green, toylike bungalows, factory sheds, paths fanning out like lines on a palm. We would go to Nirvana Café, a pretty log cabin hanging by the side of

Hermitage Road. The window-side tables offered a great view of the tea gardens below. We would see women working waist-deep in bushes.

During the seventies, this little café was the haunt of hippies. Twenty years later, it was still very popular among young European backpackers. The café had unpainted pinewood walls adorned with tantric prints and minimalist bamboo furniture. It served excellent, if overpriced, tea in painted Chinese cups, and a variety of soups and thukpa. Nirvana Café was later closed down by the authorities when a drug-dealing racket was unearthed there.

My acquaintance with Julia helped me know Darjeeling more intimately. She viewed the town built by her own countrymen from a perspective that I did not have. Her keen eyes would seek out interesting parallels, mimicry and parody in this mirage of a Scottish Arcadia that had been fabricated in the nineteenth century on a Himalayan mountain slope. Before I met her, I used to grope my way through the mist of trite nostalgia; Julia offered me bifocals.

'If you ever visit the English countryside, you'll get an idea of how homesick the founders of Darjeeling must have been. Perhaps a brief visit won't help, you'll have to live there for long. Only then will you be able to feel the depth of solitude these men suffered. Don't we face our true selves when we move out of home and go to live in a faraway land? And what is this self, by the way? An identity? But isn't that a label an outsider sticks on you? Before the Europeans came to these shores, did your forefathers ever say, "I am an Indian?" Perhaps they would have said, "I am a Hindu Brahmin belonging to such-and-such a village in such-and-such a clan." Take the Lepchas, for example. Or the Lapcheys, as the Nepalis call them. This, too, is a name thrust upon them by outsiders. Lepchas call themselves Rong, the word "lepcha" means nonsense speech. Calling a language nonsensical babble is a means to disclaim the culture of the people who speak it, to shut them out, perhaps even to deny them basic human dignity. Don't you think so?'

I nodded my head silently. Julia talked, I listened. We had been doing this for two hundred years.

Meanwhile, fog had billowed up from the valley and drawn a screen over the tea garden below. On the distant hillside, a patch of sunlight glimmered briefly upon a grove of lance-shaped pines, a network of foot tracks came alive like serpents as diaphanous clouds passed over them. The tea-plucker women had vanished into thin air. Now daylight dimmed inside the café, the windowpanes turned into opaque rectangles. The empty teacups lay on the table before us like a pair of curled-up cats. Julia's metal eardrops, newly bought on the Chowrasta footpath, glistened in the pale shadow. A faint perfume hung in the air. A Tibetan prayer song was being played at low volume on a music system. A group of young Scandinavians sporting tattered jeans, tattoos and matted hair sat around a corner table. Their bared, tanned limbs glowed in the semi-darkness like red-hot metal in an ironsmith's workshop. Printed on Julia's T-shirt, Buddha's elongated eyes gazed out convexly from over her breasts.

I don't know where Julia is now. I don't know where to find her among the eighteen million results that pop up whenever I google her name. After all these years, whenever I think of her, an image comes to my mind: that of a blonde-haired girl with green eyes out to catch a rainbow with a butterfly net.

∽

As an ethnic group, the history of the Lepchas is a story of uprooting. Before the British came, the wooded hills in this Himalayan region were theirs. The deep communion they had with nature – with its plants, animals, insects, seeds, water and stones – is celebrated in their Rongring language, one of the oldest living languages in the world.

And yet, this rich allegorical language has been dubbed as incoherent prattle, 'lepcha', and the people who speak it have been given this name. The language is dying. With it are dying, among other things, countless expressions of water that are mostly untranslatable into other tongues. But in a place where water is scarce, who cares? Of the six-thousand-odd languages spoken on earth, nearly 90 per cent have died, or are dying.[1]

Anthropologists claim that the Lepchas migrated to this region from the north of Tibet at the dawn of civilization. But Julia said that there is another opinion, according to which they came here via the land that is now part of Thailand and Myanmar. Their habitat once stretched along these mountain ranges for a length of about 200 kilometres, across the watersheds of the Koshi and Teesta – altogether about 4 million acres. Around three hundred years ago, a series of attacks by the Tibetans pushed them from fertile river valleys to the high, forested mountainsides; their territory began to shrink. In 1706, Bhutan annexed a vast area east of the river Teesta, including Kalimpong. And then, in 1835, the Rajah of Sikkim gifted the Darjeeling hills to the British. The founding of the sanatorium and the new tea gardens began to draw different communities in large numbers. For the Lepchas of Darjeeling, this led to another phase of dispossession and adjustment. Their ethnic identity, too, began to get diluted through intermarriages with other hill tribes. Lawrence Waddell, explorer and army surgeon, noted with anxiety that they were 'losing their identity by the extensive absorption of their women into the Bhotiya and Limboo tribes, with who they freely intermarry.'[2] In the eyes of the Empire-builders, the Lepchas degenerated into a slothful, cowering tribal group. Some of the photographs taken during this period, often as part of anthropological studies, of listless Lepcha men and women lounging on the ground and looking vacantly at the camera, attest to this view.

Such branding possibly had roots in unpleasant experiences. Even after Darjeeling came into their hands, the British had failed to secure full control over the local Lepcha population. They had been the subjects of the Rajah of Sikkim for generations; they had no reason to shift their fealty to the new foreign rulers. An interesting incident narrated by an English traveller in a letter written in 1839 sheds light on this:

> Whilst at Pudumtam we witnessed a scene which strongly illustrated the independent and hospitable character of the Lepchas. Two official chuprassees, deputed by Colonel Lloyd, arrived at the Dingpun's house with a copy of the proclamation, announcing the taking possession by the British Government of all the territory between the Balasun and Mahananda, ceded by the Sikkim Rajah, but by some omission or mischance, this British proclamation was unaccompanied by corresponding announcement from the Rajah to the people of the portion ceded. The Dingpun received the men hospitably, and being unable, from our residence with him, to find them accommodation in his own house, he loaded them with rice, Indian corn, chillies, tobacco etc. almost enough for a fortnight's supply, and sent them to a neighbour. But he positively refused to receive the proclamation, and on the following morning repeated the refusal, declining even to allow of its being posted against the wall of his house, although he read and explained it to his neighbours, whom he summoned for the purpose. His argument against receiving it was plainly and boldly set forth, grounded on the fact that he and his father before him, had duly and faithfully served the Maharajah, from whom they had received favours, and that therefore he could receive no other master without the Rajah's orders. Besides, he added, 'When I go to visit my maharaja, he receives me gladly and feeds me well; but if ever I pay the Colonel Sahib a visit, he gives me nothing to put in my mouth; although,

when the sahib-log or their visitors come to my village, I give them what I can and pay them every attention.[3]

After the British took over Darjeeling, their relationship with the Rajah of Sikkim quickly deteriorated. This had an impact on the Lepchas here – it became difficult to draft labourers from among them. Their response to the twin colonial enterprises of urbanization and tea gardens unfolding in the hills was cold, even hostile.

For generations, the Lepchas depended on forests for their livelihood: they collected fruits, edible roots and mushrooms, they hunted birds and small animals. They also undertook some swidden cultivation by clearing patches of forests and grew maize and other vegetables. After farming a tract of land for a few years, when the fertility of soil depleted, they shifted their settlements. Naturally, there was no proper land-revenue system in the kingdom of Sikkim. Taxes were settled according to the size of a household, not the size of land it farmed. Thus the material life of the Lepchas was governed by their need, not greed or profit.

But the new British rulers had no interest in such a system because there was no scope for revenue growth. Also, they saw the forests as an economic resource; the slash-and-burn method of cultivation was anathema to them. There was a third reason: it was nearly impossible to set up a proper administrative system among a semi-nomadic people.

The people who migrated from Nepal best suited the interests of the new rulers. They were hard-working, resourceful, obedient and skilled agriculturalists. Like Aladdin's genie, they transformed the densely forested mountainsides into terraced fields in no time. The change was so dramatic that, as early as in 1899, Lawrence Waddell was writing, 'Whole forests have been annihilated, leaving here and there only a solitary tree or narrow belts of trees in the ravines, as evidence of the magnificent woods which have fallen a sacrifice to advancing cultivation.'[4]

The destruction of forests marked the end of the distinctive ways of life of the Lepchas. The community remained, but the umbilical cord which had bound them to nature had snapped.

~

From the time that the British colonization of the Darjeeling hills had turned the Lepchas into marginal people to when Julia Griffith arrived to study their life and culture, more than a century had elapsed. Great changes had taken place during this period. With so many communities having different languages, culture and food habits living in close proximity for such a long time, a new composite social group had emerged. The process had been quite rapid, and had radical aspects. In 1907, L.S.S. O'Malley was writing in the district gazetteer:

> [The] caste system is however by no means strict among the Nepalese domiciled in Darjeeling, where the Brahman may be found working as a cultivator, a labourer or even as a *sais*. There is an extraordinary laxity in ceremonial observance; they will eat and drink things which are an abomination to the orthodox Hindu of the plains, and many of them are great flesh-eaters, relishing even beef or pork.[5]

It should be remembered that the people O'Malley was writing about migrated from deeply caste-ridden societies. When they came to settle in the new hill station of Darjeeling, not only did they leave behind immovable assets, like land and houses, but also those aspects of their culture that were static and unyielding. Or, like the ancestral copperware in Newton's house, they were brought here only to be kept in glass cases, as antique bric-a-brac, to allow them to be covered by the patina of time.

The indigenous Lepchas here also underwent great changes. With the loss of forests, the loss of a way of life that had evolved since ancient times, they became exiles in their own land. With the passage of time, intermarriages with other communities let the patina grow over their language and customs as well.

～

One day, Julia brought the news of a Lepcha settlement deep inside the Singalila forests, near the India–Nepal border. The people there still followed age-old patterns of life, she said, and lived on forest produce and a rudimentary form of agriculture. They shifted their dwellings from time to time to avoid harassment at the hands of the forest guards. She had picked up this information at Nirvana Café, from the brother-in-law of the café-owner, who organized camping trips for foreigners in the Sandakphu region. It was possible to reach the primitive settlement after a couple of days' trek through the forests, the agency-owner had told her. He would arrange for a guide, porters, tents and other equipment. Julia had teamed up with three Belgian students to undertake the expedition.

But on the afternoon before the day of the journey, she came to my college with despair writ large on her face. The trip had been cancelled – two of the Belgians were suffering from acute Delhi belly since the night before. Would I care to accompany her? she asked me point-blank.

It was an exciting offer. By then, my stay in Darjeeling had stretched to more than a few years but I had never been on a long trek in the mountains. Getting leave from college, too, was not a problem. It lay elsewhere: the price of the eight-day tour the agency was quoting per person was in dollars; converted into Indian currency, it amounted to nearly a month's salary for me. Besides, Hemraj was present in my office that afternoon. He, too, was excited about Julia's proposal because a rare subspecies of the Himalayan salamander was found in that particular forest region. Though I would be able to scrape together the money for my trip, Hemraj couldn't.

I mumbled excuses, skirting the main issue. But Julia had the proverbial Anglo-Saxon directness which could cut a path through all the forests and seas of the world. She quickly picked apart my middle-class Bengali obfuscation. 'Are you thinking about the money?' she asked me. 'I know they are charging a lot. But you see, I don't have many more days left in India, and I really need this trip to wrap up my work here. So, if you don't mind, I'd like to share part of the cost of your trip, both of you. I'll pay from my project fund.'

But Hemraj and I protested. I didn't have the physique or training to be her bodyguard, I said. And Hemraj had his own project.

We continued to bicker until Hemraj suggested a way out. We could organize the trip on our own – hire tents, sleeping bags and other equipment from Darjeeling, and guides and porters from Rimbik. It would cost us a fraction of the money the agency was charging.

The trek routes around Sandakphu and Phalut were not so popular in those days. The sarkari trekkers' huts stood burnt and ravaged in forest clearings as mute reminders of the recent agitation. The office of the state tourism department on Nehru Road gave us only a sketchy not-to-scale map of the region. Armed with a letter from our principal, Hemraj managed to borrow a pair of two-men tents, three sleeping bags, mats and a Primus stove from the Himalayan Mountaineering Institute. It took a couple of days for Julia to obtain a protected-area permit from the foreigners' registration office on Laden La Road. The purpose of our trip was kept secret. We told everyone that we were going on a pleasure trek in the Phalut region. A colleague, a professor of Botany, lent me a raincoat; it turned out to be very useful. We collected most of our rations from Darjeeling. This included two dozen packets of Maggi noodles and four chickens, dressed and coated with turmeric.

We set out on the morning of Tuesday, 11 September. A bank of grey fog was settling over the chowk as we climbed into the service jeep to Rimbik. Spotting Julia, a fake blind beggar screwed up an eye towards Golghar Restaurant and intoned in English, 'Help me pleeze! Poor b'line beggar!'

～

Elise Boulding, a well-known sociologist, set up an organization that has been compiling a database of the twenty-five most non-violent, peaceful societies on earth. The list includes a number of small communities, from the Inuits of the Arctic to the islanders of Tahiti, among whom Gauguin spent the most creative phase of his life. The Lepchas have found a place on the list; giving them company are the Birhors of eastern India and the Ladakhis. No other country in the world has so many representatives on the list.

Jealousy and rivalry had no place in traditional Lepcha society. There was also a high degree of tolerance for differences in taste and temperament. The society valued the individuality of its members provided they were not selfish or opportunistic, and followed certain basic codes of conduct. The Lepchas believed that evil spirits were behind the violent nature of men; they even had rituals to exorcise them. Community life was sustained through mutual cooperation and exchange of free labour during the farming season. There were no prisons; expulsion from society acted as a deterrent to crime. In fact, violence has no place even in their myths and legends, where enemies are defeated by the use of intelligence, not physical prowess. The Lepchas' greatest treasure, which everyone had access to all the time, was their language. It was the repository of signifiers for the rich diversity of nature, and of imagery of the most delicate sensory perceptions. This translucent language dressed the minds of the Lepchas, while their bodies were animated by the vital forces of food and sex. By surrendering to these forces, the Lepcha became 'mutanchi rongkup rumkup'—the children of Rong and of god.

～

Fifty kilometres from Darjeeling, the motorable road ended at Rimbik, on the edge of the Singalila National Park. In those days, it was a sleepy settlement under the shadow of dense, forested mountains. We stayed in the house of a local Newari man named Shiva Pradhan. His modest wooden cottage has since been converted into a budget hotel, thanks to a favourable mention in the *Lonely Planet* travel book, whose devotees normally end their Sandakphu–Phalut trek here. But at that time it was a two-storeyed structure with a large open kitchen, a row of small cubicles and a washroom in the open courtyard. Like Aunty's Café on Kutchery Road, the key to Shiva Pradhan's success as an innkeeper lay in the art of hospitality in an authentic family ambience. A place to catch one's breath after an arduous trek and the company of a simple hill family – the combination is bound to cast an irresistible spell on travellers of this lonely planet.

We inquired about the primitive Lepcha village inside the forest. Local men at a tavern in Rimbik Bazaar confirmed its existence. It was around two days' trek from the forest village of Gurdum, they said. Shiva Pradhan arranged for a guide and two porters for our journey. Nima Sherpa, our guide, was a taciturn man of uncertain age with a pair of narrow eyes chipped into a stony face. He claimed to have taken a sahib to the colony a few years earlier.

We dined that evening in the Pradhans' large kitchen with members of his extended family. Photographs of Western visitors and warm handwritten notes in different European languages were pinned to the walls. The following morning we set out for Sirikhola.

Our journey's aim was twofold: to search out a lost tribal settlement and to collect data on a rare subspecies of salamander – an ancient tribe and a Paleolithic reptile, living fossils inscribed upon the bed of time.

∼

Julia was carrying in her knapsack a paperback titled *Himalayan Village* written by Geoffrey Gorer. Gorer, an amateur anthropologist, spent four months in a Lepcha settlement in Sikkim in the 1930s. The traditional Lepcha society, as Gorer observed, seemed to enjoy a fair amount of sexual freedom within certain taboos. One could have consensual sex with almost anyone, except with members of nine generations from the mother's side and four generations from the father's side. Again, a father and son were forbidden to have sex with the same woman; the same applied to a mother and daughter with respect to a man. It was the duty of the parents to caution their pubescent children about the persons they had sex with.

There was no embarassment or shame in this but, as Gorer writes, 'Incest for the Lepchas is horrifying; they do not call it a sin but *namtoak*, an act which produces a year of disaster for the community.'[6] There was also no big fuss about a child's identity, unless it was the fruit of incest. A Lepcha boy was allowed to have sex with the wives of his brothers and uncles, if the uncles were younger than his father. The same applied to women in similar relations. Gorer had found that the Lepchas made full use of these contingencies. The casual encounters of the body never involved any emotion: no strings were attached, and there was no fuss. But, at the same time, there was nothing saturnalian about these matters. Sexual trysts – Gorer's Christian mindset called them 'legalised adultery' – usually took place in forests around the villages, behind boulders and in watch-sheds in the fields. It followed certain codes of conduct; indiscretion was socially condemned. The words of a villager named Chudo are illuminating in this context:

> If I caught Chimpet (the son of his elder brother Tafoor) sleeping with my wife I shouldn't be cross at all; on the contrary I should be very pleased, for she would be teaching him how to do it properly and I would know that he was in the hands of a good

teacher! On the other hand, if I caught a married man, who had a right to sleep with my wife, doing so, I should reproach them for their lack of shame in doing in my presence what might better be done in my absence.[7]

The Lepchas with whom Gorer lived had embraced Buddhism more than two centuries earlier. But their life was still under the influence of various ghosts and demons. The lamas had no authority over the village shamans. They would sacrifice yaks and hold communal feasts to exorcise and appease the supernatural powers. Each clan would have its own power to protect it. At the individual level, too, man and woman would be possessed by separate powers, which were passed on from father to son and from mother to daughter. Women were also ruled by Ami-rum, the god of riches, and Katong Fi, a mysterious demigod who appeared during menstruation and copulated with them in their dreams. If Katong Fi failed to visit them, it was believed that death was imminent. The woman would then retire into the forest, bathe in a mountain spring and wait for the assignation with Katong Fi, or death.

~

Dewdrops fell from low moss-covered branches, a stone loosened by a boot rolled away, fog swirled in clumps of rhododendrons, a raven cawed. An eerie silence, save the crunch of gravel under the plastic sandals of the porters. The forest was like Nima Sherpa's face, mute and impassive.

We spent the second night in Gurdum.

From Rimbik, the trail up to Sirikhola was mostly flat, along a forest of tall conifers, and strewn with smooth boulders. The Siri spring murmured across it to meet the Rammam river a few hundred feet below. A pretty log cabin with sloping double roofs stood by it. This was the trekkers' hut. A narrow hanging bridge spanned the stream. The place echoed with the ceaseless noise of water rushing into the gorge below. Tiny fire-engine-red birds flitted over the spray and darted to the wet glistening stones. They were catching insects.

'Those are scarlet minivets,' Hemraj said.

Julia rushed to the stream bed, sat on her haunches and dipped her fingers in the cold water.

'Shouldn't we have spent the night here, instead of Rimbik?' she shouted over the roar of rapids, pointing to the trekkers' hut. Seen from the edge of the stream, glowing in the light reflected off the water, it appeared like a mystic Japanese pagoda.

'But then we wouldn't have found the porters here,' I replied. 'And we would have been like the poor creatures over there!'

I pointed towards the bridge. A pack of six mules, loaded with huge sacks, had appeared from a bridle track behind the cabin and were now gingerly stepping on to the hanging bridge in single file. A boy, wearing a coarse Tibetan coat and a red cap, egged them on with a stick.

The bridge, the mountain spring, the animals, the boy and the log cabin in the background – a perfect picture postcard. Julia whistled in joy and ran to fetch the camera from her knapsack. Frames were captured in succession: the mule caravan at the head of the bridge, upon the bridge, away from the bridge.

After drinking mugs of hot salt-tea that the caretaker of the trekkers' hut made for us, we took the bridle path. A steep climb began. Keeping the cascading stream to the left, the path wound up through a thick sun-dappled forest of firs, magnolias and yellow primroses glowing in the thickets. After an ascent of nearly two hours, we came to a wide ledge in the mountain and found the burnt remains of trees standing like giant spears. Nothing grew on the dry grass. Hemraj broke off a piece of charcoal and sniffed it.

'There was a forest fire here before the rains,' he said.

The National Park rules had banned the collection of dry leaves and twigs by villagers living on the margins of the park. During spring, when deciduous trees shed their leaves, the forest waits for a spark to turn it into a devastating fire. We would find more such forest areas later, blackened and deathly, in the higher reaches.

Gurung herders grazed their yaks at a height of ten to twelve thousand feet. Chhurpi, a type of dessicated cheese, is made from the milk of these animals and sold in the markets of Darjeeling and Kalimpong. This practice has been going on since the British times. The founders of Darjeeling had realized early that it would not make economic sense to procure from distant plains the regular supply of dairy products the sanatorium would need. It was necessary to have large grazing grounds nearby to meet the requirements of fodder and firewood – in short, a reserve forest. With this aim, vast tracts of forestland were bought up in 1882–83 from the descendants of a wealthy nobleman named Chebu Lama. Woodcutters and cattle-grazers were settled there. After Independence and the passing of forest-protection laws, these villages remained but the people living there lost their rights over the produce of the surrounding forests.

Gurdum was one such village.

We reached up there from Sirikhola but, as Nima told us, trekkers usually came here on the last leg of the Sandakphu–Phalut trek. From Sandakphu top, off the spur that connects Phalut, a trail climbs down the steep hillside clad in silver fir and other subalpine trees and leads to the village. Here, board and lodging was available for trekkers in a loghouse that hung over the deep gorge of the Siri. Surrounded by dense forests, Gurdum was alive with the muffled roar of rapids and fleecy mists rising from below. A dozen Bhutia families lived here, rearing cattle and farming maize and other vegetables in tiny forest clearings. Their huts, made of wood and corrugated tin, stood on stilts against the hillside. Pigs and poultry were raised under living quarters; the cattle-sheds were open on all sides and made of dried leaves woven on wooden frames. Clumps of prayer flags fluttered here and there. At the approach to the village was a row of sacred Mani stones.

We pitched our tents above the dwellings upon a grassy clearing on the edge of a rhododendron grove. But the dinner that evening was arranged at the village headman's house. The special favour was granted us because of the blonde memsahib in our group.

The main room of the headman's house, around fifty feet long and twenty feet wide, was built out of solid pine logs. The walls inside were burnished with years of oily soot while, outside, the barks were alive with layers of moss. A hearth made of stone and mud was built on a part of flattened hillside flush with the wooden floor of the room. Visitors were invited to sit near it for the warmth.

Despite his boyish looks, the headman had a large family of several children and grandchildren. Members of the village council were also present, huddled near the fire and chatting among themselves. I couldn't follow their conversation, and asked Hemraj about it.

'In these remote places, they often mix their dialects with Nepali or Tibetan,' he said. 'Some of the expressions are so localized that they sometimes differ on two sides of the same mountain.'

'Can you mark the differences?' I asked him.

'Of course not!' Hemraj smiled. 'I'm also fumbling along.'

But Julia wasn't bothered. She had already cosied up to the womenfolk using the language of signs and touch. They giggled and tittered as they compared notes on skin colour and hair, clothing and ornaments. The headman's wife, a matronly woman in an apron-like dress with horizontal stripes, handed us tongba in bamboo-stem vessels even as she tended the fire in the hearth. A large kettle of water hung over it. One only needed to fill up the bamboo vessels to have an endless drinking session. There was enough supply of fermented millet in a large wooden cask.

About four feet above the oven that burned day and night like Ravana's funeral pyre, slabs of cheese wrapped in gunny were drying upon a wooden frame. There were also strips of salted yak meat, bundles of corn, strings of onions and garlic, bamboo shoots, dalle khursani (arguably the hottest variety of chilli in the world) and other dried herbs and vegetables. Freshly harvested potatoes were heaped in a corner, next to upright wood. A baby swaddled in sheepskin slept on the raised wooden floor. A large grey dog, its eyes alert under droopy lids, lay close and gave it warmth. All the social and biological needs of a family were laid out around the hearth, its heat and scented smoke.

After all these years, the word hearth still calls up to my mind that room in the headman's house. I can vividly recall the knots on neatly dovetailed planks, the simple furniture bearing kukri marks, the carved wooden bowls and the weave on the yak-hair rug – the work of brawny arms and deft fingers.

I also recall a face – prematurely wrinkled, framed in a worn woollen cap, lit up like an ancient folktale by the flickering light from the fire. His name was Pemba and he was a shepherd who lived on the other side of the mountain, a full day's trek away. He had come to Gurdum to receive an old umbrella that had belonged to his uncle, also a shepherd. The uncle had declared once he died, the umbrella should go to Pemba. The old man had recently passed away, and Pemba had come to collect his bequest.

Pemba was sitting in a corner of the room, eating roasted potatoes with cheese chutney. He bowed nervously whenever our eyes met. I learnt that he had set out before dawn from his village to arrive late in the afternoon, and would depart soon. He would walk through the night around the forested spur and reach his village the following morning. When we wanted to see the umbrella, Pemba jumped to his feet, shuffled forward and held it in his outstretched hands like a sacred object. It was a large umbrella, of faded, patched-up cloth sewn upon a framework of canes. The canes had been replaced many times over. Perhaps the uncle, too, had inherited the umbrella from an ancestor. Now it was Pemba's and would go to an heir after him. The cloth and the canes would be replaced from time to time, but the umbrella would remain the same and be passed on from generation to generation. Not an article made of cloth and canes, but an idea; not a faith or a myth, but the shadow of an object that was an integral part of a shepherd's life; a shadow imbued with the scents of the sun and rains, not sacred flowers and blood.

After dinner, Hemraj and I took leave of the headman's family to spend the night in our tent above the village. Julia stayed back at the behest of the womenfolk. Pemba followed us. We would have to set out very early the following morning, Nima informed us. But the people we talked to in the village didn't have encouraging words. No one had seen or heard about the settlement we were searching for. Perhaps it had been there in the past, and had moved to more remote forests in Nepal. The news cast shadows of despair over Julia's face. But Nima was impassive.

'We'll start very early tomorrow,' he said. 'We'll have to cut our path through dense jungle. There is no route.'

Pemba bade us farewell near the tents and disappeared into the dark stands of rhododendron. With the big umbrella resting upon his shoulder, a kukri on his waist, bits of chhurpi in his pocket and a talisman on his neck, he would cross the deep nocturnal forest to go to the other side of the mountain. The chhurpi, kukri and the talisman would protect him from thirst, wild animals and ghosts respectively.

We, on the other hand, had lots of equipment scattered around our tents. Two single-hoop tents stood side by side in the clearing – one for Julia and the other for Hemraj and myself. Julia's tent was empty. The lights of the village below had gone out and the dwellings were lost in darkness. A lone dog barked there from time to time. Countless stars shone above in the clear sky. A mountain spur jutted before us and looked like the hairy back of a primeval animal. The subalpine forest started from here: bamboo, birch, rhododendron and, higher up, rows of spear-shaped silver firs. Above their pointed heads the Milky Way stretched across the horizon, packed with millions of stars, and a big comet close by. The comet, tinted green like Julia's eyes, looked out of the bottomless depths in search of a lost tribal settlement.

∼

It was the Hale–Bopp comet, I later learnt, that was visible to the naked eye throughout that year. Never had a comet been seen for so long, from both the hemispheres, since 1811. The closer it had come to the sun, the more luminous it had become, and had grown a pair of tails – one composed of bluish-green gas and turned away from the sun, the other aligned to its orbit and made of yellow interstellar dust.

The bright comet visible in the night sky all over the earth spread panic among various communities. One of them was a California-based occult group named Heaven's Gate, whose members believed that a spaceship from another galaxy was hovering behind the comet's tail. They were convinced that the time had come for the destruction of planet Earth; the only way out was to quit it. The intergalactic spaceship was waiting there to transport the souls of willing humans to a higher plane of existence. For this mission, the members of Heaven's Gate gathered in an upscale San Diego apartment on a spring afternoon. They recorded their last hours on video, narrating their objectives, and committed mass suicide.

The bodies were recovered on 26 March 1997. They had consumed orange juice to cleanse their system before the final act, after which they had injected themselves with phenobarbital mixed with vodka. They did not commit suicide together but divided themselves into small groups; each successive group neatly laid out the bodies of fellow members. They wore identical black dresses, Nike sneakers and armbands that read HEAVEN'S GATE AWAY TEAM.

Lepchas do not believe that souls leave this planet after death. In north Sikkim, inside the Kanchenjunga Biosphere Reserve, is the Dzongu Valley. Covered in pristine forests, the valley is ringed with tall mountains, washed with countless springs and endowed with rich biodiversity. The river Teesta flows through it. For generations of Lepchas diffused all over the world, this is their spiritual home. Ten years after the appearance of the Hale–Bopp comet, engineers of the National Hydel Power Corporation turned up, like comets from outer space, in the Dzongu Valley to set up a series of power plants. This set off protest movements across the valley; several Lepcha organizations from Sikkim and Darjeeling joined in. The identity of the tribe was at stake, they were committed to stop the ravages on their sacred reserve at all costs.

～

After the night in Gurdum, the weather began to turn forbidding. Dense fog swelled up from the gorge and cast a pall over the forests. Visibility was so poor that it was difficult to see anything two feet away. It became quite a challenge to hack our path through thickets of bamboo that covered the steep mountainside. Water dripped ceaselessly from the trees overhead. At ten thousand feet, the ground was surprisingly soft and clayish; it made walking difficult in this wet weather. We almost crawled, and hauled ourselves up by clutching at the roots of rhododendrons. With each gasping breath, fine particles of water seemed to fill our lungs. After every few steps they felt like they would burst. Nima, steady as a ramrod and unmoved by our plight, stopped from time to time and searched for old signs on tree trunks. Sometimes he cupped his palm around the mouth and ululated to communicate with the porters who had overtaken us.

Responses echoed back through the mists. Weak daylight drifted through moss-covered branches like coils of smoke.

And then a chill wind rose to freeze the mist and turn it into sleet. Within minutes, the ground and the trees were covered with white feathery pellets. It was a beautiful sight, but the slushy forest floor made our advance extremely difficult. Water seeped in through the shoes and turned the feet numb with cold. I cursed myself for getting into this crazy venture.

After nearly three hours of this, it seemed we had crossed the border into Nepal. This would mean trouble if a forest guard spotted us because Julia didn't have a permit to enter the country. But Nima was, as usual, unperturbed. He showed us the dry bed of a spring and declared, 'Nepal is on the other side.'

'You mean to say this far is India? Is that the border with India?' Julia exclaimed, stopping in her tracks and taking out her camera. The exhaustion on her face had suddenly been replaced with a flush of strange excitement.

I failed to understand her odd behaviour that day. Many years later, on seeing a group of young British trekkers hugging and kissing a squat basalt milestone on top of Phalut, and taking photographs of themselves, I understood.

Phalut is that point on the map where the borders of West Bengal, Sikkim and Nepal meet. Before Sikkim became part of India in 1975, this was the meeting point of three countries and, before that, the border of the British Empire in the subcontinent. A milestone demarcated it on the bare, windswept mountaintop in Phalut. For an Indian like me, it was impossible to guess the feelings the ordinary-looking milestone evoked in a British tourist, feelings of boundless ambition and drive that, for centuries, coursed through the veins of a race.

Just as the stone at Phalut had become a totem of racial identity for those trekkers, the dry spring-bed became for Julia – in spite of it possibly being a fiction invented by Nima – a cherished line of history.

Late in the afternoon, we reached a broad shelf in the mountain to find the footprints of a bear. A forest of silver firs rose above; stretched below were dense thickets of slender bamboos, the habitat of the Himalayan red panda. We climbed another two hundred feet or so to come to a pokhri of dark water. On its edge stood a neat pile of stones of what looked like a chorten, paint-peeled and lichen-spotted, its reflection shimmering in the water.

'The settlement should be somewhere near this,' Nima said at last, pointing to the chorten.

Julia's forehead was creased with suspicion.

'But that's a Buddhist shrine!' she said, disconcerted. 'The people I'm searching for aren't supposed to come under the influence of Buddhism. They are animists. They would have their traditional priests, bongthings and muns, but not the lamas.'

I interposed, 'But Buddha's teachings have spread all over the Himalayas. Do you think it is possible for a human group, howsoever cut off it may be from civilization, not to come in contact with them?'

Julia stood silently before the pile of stones. Her eyes had turned opaque like the water of the pokhri. Wet strands of hair clung to the back of her neck. She looked deeply exhausted and at a loss.

'Perhaps you are right,' she said finally. 'The Lepchas came in contact with the Buddhist missionaries from Tibet in the seventeenth century. It's been such a long time. But do you know something? The more their societies have come under the influence of the lamas, the more their roots have withered. An organized religion can do to a society what a civilization cannot. Civilization has only a superficial influence, but religion changes man from the inside.'

Be it a café in Darjeeling or deep in the mountains, Julia would be the speaker and I the listener – always. But Hemraj had no such covenant. He had begun his investigation right at the moment he had set his eyes on the pokhri. He was now lying flat on his chest on the edge of the pool and probing the water with a twig. A few feet away, one of the porters had propped the load on his back against a boulder, taken off the head-strap and was wiping the sweat on his face with a rag. Nima sat on his haunches and calmly crushed tobacco on his palm.

'Did you find anything?' I asked Hemraj.

'They breed in this water, but now they are not here. At this altitude their hibernation begins early.'

I slipped the knapsack off my shoulders and stretched flat on my back upon dry grass. As I lay still, I could feel the sharp cold biting into my flesh. My fingers and toes were turning numb.

Suddenly I heard Julia scream, 'O my god! O my god!' We rushed to find her frantically thrashing her legs. She had taken off her shoes and rolled up the trousers. There, between the toes and the knees, dozens of leeches squirmed on every inch of her exposed ivory skin. The dribbles of blood glistened.

As I reached out to pluck off the leeches, Nima stopped me. He brought his face close to her legs and began to spit bits of tobacco upon them. The wriggly creatures began to drop off instantly and the bleeding stopped. Soon, Julia's legs were a mess of blood and brown spittle. The horror and repugnance that rioted upon her face is indescribable, but not unfamiliar. I have seen Bengali girls react in the same way at the sight of a cockroach or a spider. But never a memsahib.

'Tobacco is the best antidote against these tiger leeches,' Hemraj said. 'They have an anaesthetic chemical in their saliva that they inject into their victim's bloodstreams.'

From a plastic bag, he now carefully pulled out an object that nearly pushed Julia into another fit. The two porters laughed at her reaction.

'Pani kukur! Pani kukur!' they said reassuringly. Waterdog!

A full-sized salamander, dead, hung from between Hemraj's fingers. Apart from the distension from being in water for so long, it was intact. It seemed to be sleeping the long winter sleep.

'Do they call salamanders waterdogs?' I asked.

'Yes, because sometimes they snap their jaws on the surface of water and emit tiny barking sounds,' Hemraj said.

I had seen the creatures from a distance in murky water or half concealed in wet moss. I had never had the chance to see one up close. This one was about six inches long, blackish brown, with a flattened head, a serrated tail and a double row of glands along the vertebra: altogether an ugly little species suspended for two billion years like a hyphen between the reptile and the mammal.

'This one is full-grown,' Hemraj said. 'It had come to the pokhri during the summer season for mating, but couldn't return to its nesting place in time because winter has set in early this year. The water in the pokhri freezes at night now.'

Could the clock that had been ticking for two billion years in the genes ever blunder? What if the newt had refused to leave the pool, despite the growing cold, and retreated to its cosy winter haunt in the crack of a stone or a bamboo culm? What if it had failed to find a mate, and waited and waited, even after the allotted season had come to an end? Perhaps, as it waited, it felt the spiderwebs of ice spread around its puny body, felt the fatal cold pierce through the soft skin of its belly and the knobby glands on its back, and yet it persevered until the procreative heat succumbed to the chill of death.

We pitched our tents near the pokhri. The clouds began to fade away soon after the sun set, and dark wooded mountains around us appeared on all sides. On a bare vertical cliffside lit up by the last rays of the sun, gaunt silver firs clung to reddish volcanic rock that lay in horizontal folds like giant books on a shelf. Now a crisp wind rose and birdsong could be heard for the first time in the day. Flocks of parrotbills were flying over the mist-hazed forest a couple of thousand feet below us; they were like shoals of fish swimming against the tide over dark green moss. The gathering darkness in a forest of rhododendron sparkled with the plumes of golden-breasted babblers. The evening was drawing on, the clouds continued to settle, and soon a fleecy carpet was formed down below, with the mountaintops rising above it like icebergs. The stars came out in the sky, and the comet Hale–Bopp, its tails touched by the glimmer of the sun that had already set.

The porters gathered lots of pine cones and twigs and made a bonfire. As the oil-rich cones burst into flames, they lit up the network of pale branches in the forest above. We proceeded to roast the chickens. Nima was cooking a khichri made of rice and tinned beans in a pressure cooker. Hemraj had bought Sikkimese brandy in Rimbik Bazaar. It was named Fireball, and the bottle was encased in a red plastic ball. The liquid fire joined the wood fire and gave the fierce cold a tough fight. The ensuing heat seemed to calm Julia's leech-stung nerves.

'Let's have some songs now!' she announced and started to prod Hemraj and me.

I couldn't sing, but Hemraj sang a Gorkhali song he had learnt as a Boy Scout. Then Julia sang an Irish folk song to the accompaniment of clapping.

The two porters were sitting across the fire, listening. The verve in the memsahib's song was infectious, and one of them began to sing a local song in a high-pitched voice. It fanned out into the surrounding mountainscape.

And then it happened. Across the chorten was a stretch of scrubland that rose up to a ridge. A line of silver firs stood upon its crest and concealed the endless expanse beyond. None of us had noticed the clouds blow away from there. Now we saw, behind the silhouette of trees, the Kanchenjunga in all its glory under the blue astral light.

I have seen this great snow-clad range so many times from so many different locations in the Himalayas. I have seen it painted in lithographs, aquatints, watercolours and gouache, and also in innumerable photographs taken since the late nineteenth century. But the Kanchenjunga I saw that evening was truly incomparable. Its beauty left us speechless – and meditative. We sat outside in the freezing cold even after dinner was over, as close to the dying embers as possible, our eyes transfixed on the silvery ranges.

Most of our life is made up of restless expectancy for the future and a wistful attachment to the past. Very rarely do we live fully in the present. That evening, it seemed we had shed the scales of desire and nostalgia from our consciousness and were plunging into the everlasting moment of a glowing present.

By this time Julia had realized that there was no Lepcha settlement caught in a time warp inside the forest, none that we could hope to find. But not a trace of dejection was visible. Looking out at the Kanchenjunga, she narrated to me the life story of Alexander Csoma de Kőrös, about how the call of the unknown had drawn this Hungarian away from his family and country to surrender himself to the search for a world of knowledge preserved in an obscure language.

'I always used to wonder what it was for which a person could wager one's life? I think I've found the answer after I came to India. It is this urge to see life from a different viewpoint. It is these ways of seeing that are the crucial thing. Otherwise, life is the same, everywhere it is the same. Isn't it? After this night, every time you'll see Kanchenjunga in the future, in all the different views you'll have of it from all the different places, this view here will remain inside your eyes like a lingering shadow.'

Under a moonless, star-spangled sky, the snow-capped peaks were emanating a pale blue glow. They evoked a terrifying beauty in the surrounding mountainscape.

'There was something in the traditional Lepcha way of life that I find rather mystifying,' I said. 'There was no place for sexual jealousy, it seems. How easily one could share one's partner with another person. But that didn't lead to debauchery, the society was governed by codes of conduct. In our Mahabharata, too, there is the story of five brothers sharing a woman among themselves. But that is an exception. The disrobing of Draupadi stirs up jealousy, and that leads to violence.'

'That is the essence of all great epics – sexual jealousy, kidnapping, rape and warfare,' Julia said.

'And not just the epics,' I added. 'Sexual jealousy is the driving force of our modern culture, isn't it? From Joyce's *Ulysses* to a motorcycle ad, it's always there. The societies that have been able to conquer this will remain free from violence. We don't need a Freud to tell us this.'

We had a long chat that night. It was so cold that my fingers, toes and the tip of my nose began to ache. And yet, neither of us could tear ourselves away from the great beauty in front of us and get into the tents. Hemraj, Nima and the porters had already retired into their sleeping bags.

The embers died and the icy cold pounced on us with the ferocity of a tiger. Julia, too, crawled back to her tent. She was probably writing her diary under a torchlight; her hunched shadow wavered on the tent cloth. It brought to my mind the image of the fabled Lepcha woman keeping a vigil for Katong Fi.

The following day, a long eight-hour trek through another part of the forest brought us back to Rimbik. We returned to Darjeeling the following afternoon. News was awaiting me in college: Dadu had died the day we set out.

~

I left for home immediately. The entire road to Kurseong was covered in thick fog. After the descent to a height of about a thousand feet, the familiar trees and cottages began to appear. I could see hutments on the wayside, and bare-chested men fetching water from springs. As the vehicle negotiated the hairpin bend over the tea garden in Makaibari, the haze of endless plains stretched below: the yellow riverbeds, the forest of blossoming teaks, the neat matchboxes of the army barracks, the ludo-board roads and, in the distance, the steaming mirage of Siliguri town. After Long View tea estate, and the scattering of huts in Punkhabari, we hit, with a suddenness that has never failed to amaze me, the straight flat road across the broad expanse of tea bushes under slim acacia trees. The eyes could travel far into the distance without so much as a mound or a boulder to impede the view.

Ah the plains! The vehicle entered the tepid climate of an endless whale's stomach. At every breath, its warm gastric juices filled me up. I was born in this tropical heat, I grew up in it, my nerves and guts were attuned to this atmosphere. Whenever I returned to it after a long interval, I was always filled with a sense of deep tranquillity. To tell the truth, I felt not a shred of grief. Slowly, the honks of rickshaws on the streets of Siliguri, snatches of Bengali conversation, billboards with the Bengali script upon them brought back to me the world of sights, sounds and smells I have always known.

The fish in mustard sauce at the pice hotel behind the bus terminus was as sharp as ever; so was the East Bengal accent of the hotel's owner. I bought the morning's *Anandabazar Patrika* and waited in the lounge, sitting on a canary-yellow plastic chair nailed to the ground, for the night bus to Calcutta. An electric fan overhead flapped its weary bat wings and blew warm air. A scatter of people lounged about. Among them was a group of men with tonsured heads, deposited here by an interstate bus and waiting for another to pick them up again. A corpulent woman dressed in an orange maxi and a wet towel wrapped around her head like Egyptian headgear emerged from the Sulabh washroom. The air of the lounge was instantly suffused with the smell of sandalwood soap. My head felt heavy, my senses were dulled, the heat induced a strange voluptuousness.

This state of mind continued inside the moving bus. As it left behind the city lights of Siliguri and sped along the dark monotone of National Highway 34, I fell asleep. I woke up late at night. The bus had stopped somewhere, the seats were nearly empty. Outside, a line of vehicles waited in darkness by the side of the highway. A pair of dhabas stood cheek by jowl across the road; knots of shadowy people were moving about under glaring lightbulbs. Two thin, bare-bodied boys were engaged in a shouting match as they reeled out the names, prices and degree of hotness of the day's menu. A paan-bidi stall belted out a familiar song: 'Baazigar o baazigar…'

I walked a few paces to the edge of the road and stood under a stand of acacia trees. Sheets of water glistened below on the field, reflecting the night sky broken by stalks of paddy. Frogs croaked. Suddenly, I felt a knot in my throat. Dadu was no more. I would never be able to return to the Darjeeling I was leaving behind, where I would go back after a week of ritual mourning. One can never step into the same river twice.

~

When I came back to Darjeeling, I learnt that Julia had left. She had told me about her plans to travel to a few countries in South Asia on her way back to England. In a few weeks, I began to receive the picture postcards: Mt Annapurna reflected on the blue waters of Phewa Lake in Pokhara, Manila's velvet skyline studded with glittering skyscrapers, dolphins leaping out of a milkshake sea in Phuket, a Taiwanese tribal couple posing regally before the camera, the national monument in Kuala Lumpur … with a few quick lines scribbled at the back of these cards: 'Reached here today' ... 'It's been raining since last week' ... 'the people here use the exclamation "laa!" – just as they do in Darjeeling' ... 'missing you a lot' (me? us?) ... 'fried salamanders are sold in roadside snack joints here – please tell this to Hemraj'...

Like the comet Hale–Bopp, Julia Griffith receded. At first, the yellow tail made of the pollen of the sun faded, folded into the blue orbital tail; then, night after night, it continued to sink in the western horizon, until one day it couldn't be seen. The picture postcards stopped coming; the night skies turned darker and drained of colour.

VII

DRUMBEATS IN THE MIST

Where the summer season ends in Darjeeling and the tourists head back to the plains, that is when the town beckons me. Puffs of fog rise up from the valleys to blot out the distant views until they are stretched over the hill station. Then 'Sight Seen' taxis are put under covers, the cable cars are sent to their hangars, the stalls below Chowrasta fold up, the hotels are closed for the season. Darjeeling becomes an empty toytown.

In the middle of September, a pallid sunlight sometimes seeps in through the curtain of fog. One morning, tea-plucker women appear on the green rain-washed slopes. Another afternoon, the air is redolent with the smell of roasted corn. The clouds over the distant mountains are lacerated with a bleeding sunset. And then comes the night of the singing cicadas. The following morning is unerringly clear and, like an impetuous explosion, Kanchenjunga appears in the skies.

∼

Since my transfer to Calcutta in 1999, I had been carrying memories of Darjeeling like malarial parasites in my bloodstream. They ambushed me at unexpected moments with febrile intensity, during the invisible change of seasons in the busy city, in the scent of the first rain or a traffic-stopper fog, in the monochrome print on a packet of tea leaves or the taste of fiery chutney accompanying a plate of momos on a Chowringhee pavement. But I could not manage to go back. The opportunity came in 2006, during the Durga Puja holidays.

There is no greater luxury on earth than a return to the town of memories. No greater peril too. In Siliguri's Tenzing Norgay Bus Terminus, I searched in vain for the fleet of vintage Willys jeeps; Tata Sumo, Qualis, Scorpio and other brands of SUVs had replaced them. Siliguri, too, had spread in the last few years to the boundary of the Mahananda Wildlife Sanctuary. The road beyond Darjeeling More crossing was dotted with motels and bars – to serve, it seemed, city slickers on a long drive rather than tourists to the hills. This, combined with the new squatters' colonies and the moribund tea gardens, presented a rather grim picture. After Sukna, the forests of the death valley of the Terai appeared to have grown thinner. I felt the rush of old memories at the sharp bend in the road and the sudden ascent.

Naguib Mahfouz, the Egyptian novelist, once said in an interview about his book *The Echoes of an Autobiography* that it was not really about memories, but rather about how it felt to have them. I was trying to get a sense of that feeling when the car passed Sonada. I turned my head instinctively to the chemist's shop and got the shock of my life. Could this man at the counter be Nikhil Tamang? The vivacious young man, my first acquaintance in Darjeeling, had become grey and appeared slow and careworn. I had to take a look at myself in the car's rear-view mirror to come to terms with the shock.

On reaching Darjeeling, I had to fight an urge to get into a Siliguri-bound taxi. Could the town I had known so intimately have undergone such a harsh change, or was I mistaken? It was like the bare bones of a nostalgia whose flesh had rotted away in the tomb of memories.

It was impossible to walk through the press of people in Chowk Bazaar without bumping into someone, or being trampled upon, in the mad farrago of vehicles and vendors' carts, fast-food kiosks, shopping malls, gaping drains, dug-up roads, fire-trap tenements, skies mangled by bunches of cables, brown festering patches on the hillsides, overflowing public latrines, long familiar queues in front of the springs, piles of garbage in vacant lots, mangy dogs, crowds of patients spilling out of doctors' clinics, power cuts, generator sets spewing sooty fumes, and tourists swarming about in the forests of woollens at wayside stalls. Planters' Club, Das Studio, Glenary's, Keventers and other prominent landmarks looked dusty and lost in the suppurating tide of a different type of urbanization.

I strolled about Chowrasta and lounged on the open terrace of Keventers with a mug of coffee. Local youngsters sporting designer clothes and body jewellery occupied the tables around me. They spoke an accented Nepali thickly laced with English, called their friends in Delhi and Bangalore into the adda with a flick of the button on their expensive mobile phones.

A new generation had arrived in the hills, the legatees of the fruits of the Hill Council. They roared along stunned hill roads on their leonine sports bikes, showering mists of imported perfume from the burgundy hair of their pretty, hip-clasping pillion riders, spent endless hours at Inox, the new movie theatre, or in Shangrila bar, drinking beauty and beer. They beckoned the waiters with whistles to pay bills that could buy a month's provisions for a family living in Bhutia Bustee. Their fathers – who dressed up in safari suits and travelled in beacon-fitted SUVs – held important posts in the council, or were contractors – possibly both.

Laissez-faire economics has discovered a behavioural similarity between capital and liquid: both trickle down.

A glass of chilled beer, too, has liquid trickling down its sides. But that is the water molecules suspended in air, not the thing inside the glass. Physical science calls this process condensation. In the new Darjeeling, I found this process of condensation on the faces of young men on the streets.

The local magazines and blog forums were dripping with anger:

Why do we only protest, but can't do anything worthwhile?

Why do we look away from the pests that are feeding on our society?

Why do we keep our mouths shut even when they rob our rights from us?

Why do we give our opinions from seven hundred miles away, and write articles on the 'lost generation' and douse the fire in our heart?

Why can't we work together for a better tomorrow? Why don't our gems return home?

Why does nothing change, though we know what it is that needs to be changed?

Why do I only ask questions? I don't have an answer.

I don't have an answer, I don't have a home, I don't have an identity, I don't have a face, I don't have a heart, I don't have a soul. My self is being raped every moment, and yet I smile – the typical Darjeelingey smile. I return home with blinded eyes, shun my dear ones and exclaim, 'Abo yahan kei pani chhaina!' Nothing remains!

~

There is no greater luxury on earth than a return to the town of memories. No greater despair too. I roamed its streets aimlessly before calling on the people I had known.

Many old shops had new glass fronts; marble and granite, too, were more common now. The changing tastes of the Bengali middle class had left their marks on the wares displayed at tourist shops. The public phone booths had almost disappeared, cyber cafés had come up in their place. The old halwai shop on Laden La Road had metamorphosed into a pâtisserie.

I was climbing down the steep flight of stairs around Hayden Hall when familiar drumbeats and incense smoke hit my senses. I saw the Durga Puja pandal erected on a plot of land as always. But as

I walked up to it and peered inside, I was taken by surprise. Instead of the familiar ten-armed goddess astride her lion, there stood a rough obelisk decorated with sindoor and floral offerings.

It turned out that Goddess Durga had been worshipped in this form in Darjeeling for the past two years. A fortnight earlier, drivers and automobile mechanics had paid homage to Lord Viswakarma by worshipping their iron tools, not the usual image of the god and his elephant. Before that, Saraswati, the goddess of learning, had been invoked in large boulders transported from the riverbeds.

These events had been reported in the media as odd pieces of news but I had somehow missed them. Now I learnt that the GNLF, whose support base was eroding, had been coercing the hill people to perform these bizarre rituals because Ghising wanted to showcase Darjeeling district as a tribal area to gain the Sixth Schedule status. It followed a simple logic: tribal people who still held on to their primitive faiths worshipped stones and other inanimate objects rather than the human form. So, if these practices could be made popular here, it would give teeth to the demand for the special constitutional status. Thus went the absurd project of identity-construction for a few million people living in the Darjeeling hills. Later that year, an agreement would be signed in New Delhi to pave the way for the Sixth Schedule status. In the assembly elections the following year, the issue would help Ghising's party win all the three hill seats.

Mutton in Darjeeling was usually very tough and difficult to tenderize because of low pressure. Benson and I once gave my neighbours a sleepless night with endless whistles of the pressure cooker as we were trying to cook the meat of a particularly indomitable goat. Around midnight, we heard a knock on the door. It was my landlord, dressed in pajamas, with a few eggs in his hand. He offered me the eggs and, struggling to work up a polite smile upon a peeved face, said, 'Sir, please turn off the pressure cooker and try to make do with these eggs for dinner. You can start the whistles again in the morning. We can't sleep, you see!'

On that historic day in 1988, when the Darjeeling Gorkha Hill Council accord was being signed at the behest of the prime minister Rajiv Gandhi, West Bengal chief minister Jyoti Basu is said to have remarked to Subash Ghising with his trademark insouciance, 'Try to make do with this for now. If it doesn't work out, you might think of starting another agitation.'

But could the craving for mutton be appeased with eggs? As the inept and corrupt face of the council became known, dark vapours of frustration built up in the minds of the hill people. The political atmosphere of Darjeeling was like a pressure cooker. Sensing this, the government of West Bengal, together with Subash Ghising, hit upon a rather antiquated solution: the Sixth Schedule. As this became the talk of the town, the complicated legal provision enshrined in the Constitution was translated in the common parlance into the homespun Chhakka Shedool.

On that visit to Darjeeling, I saw the rainbow of Chhakka Shedool upon the murky clouds gathered over the mountains.

The tribal-dominated areas of Assam, Tripura, Meghalaya and Mizoram are protected under the Sixth Schedule of the Indian Constitution. The status bestows some additional administrative and economic powers to locally elected bodies. They are empowered to implement decisions in matters of education, health, land distribution, forest conservation and other welfare activities. The blueprint of the tripartite agreement between the Darjeeling Gorkha Hill Council and the central and state governments – which was being given final touches – had similar provisions.

On the face of it, everything looked fine. Who could say no if elected leaders at the local level were given more power? And even if they might turn out to be corrupt and incompetent, so what? At least they would speak the same language, they would stick around through thick and thin. At least they wouldn't offer opaque looks like the officers airdropped from Kolkata. But there was also a precarious clause in the proposed agreement: only those people of Nepali origin who fulfilled the official criteria of a scheduled tribe would be recognized as such.

What would the people of the Darjeeling hills gain from a Sixth Schedule status? What would be the fate of a large section of the population who would be denied the reservation? What would happen to the Biharis and the Marwaris who had been living there for generations and were integrated into its economy?

Subash Ghising attempted to answer these questions in his inimitable style, mixing sophistry with pure fantasy. A Sixth Schedule status would be a better bet than statehood, he claimed in public meetings. And there was nothing to worry about reservation: once the Sixth Schedule was declared, everyone would automatically become scheduled tribes. And why only people, he would go on, all the trees, birds and animals, the Darjeeling tea, the orchids of Kurseong, the snow and even the sunrise from Tiger Hill would come under the purview of constitutional reservation.

Listening to him at rallies around the town in those days was like reading from a novel. It was the autumn of the patriarch. He would go to inaugurate a water-pumping station and sing the virtues of eating bougainvillea leaves every day. Elsewhere, he would lecture on the various avatars of Goddess Chamunda. Once, on an official visit to the capital, he even threatened to raise the demand that Darjeeling be made a part of Bangladesh, as it used to be administered from East Bengal during British times. There were no permanent relief shelters for the people who became homeless due to landslips every year, but that didn't stop him from spending crores to build a grand auditorium on the Mall.

But perhaps the most bizarre thing Ghising gave Darjeeling was right in the heart of Chowrasta. A beautiful park was dug up to install a musical fountain. The viewers would buy tickets to watch the psychedelic performance that required ten thousand litres of water. Here the patriarch was like the Darjeeling version of Marie Antoinette: So what if there is no potable water at home? Let them watch jets of water dance to music!

Darjeelingeys, used to a life of grotesque paradoxes, took these things with a shrug and a smile, because, as is popularly said:

> Only in Darjeeling do people sit in dense fog and watch an entire soccer match without knowing what is happening on the field.
>
> Only in Darjeeling do you walk through town once and meet the same people ten times.
>
> Only in Darjeeling do the unemployed dress better than the employed.
>
> Only in Darjeeling do you find distance in kilometres and places in miles – Char-mile, Dus-mile, Baarah-mile, Bis-mile.
>
> Only in Darjeeling does the prettiest girl always elope with a taxi driver.
>
> Only in Darjeeling does a train get caught in a traffic jam…

But Ghising knew that he had no magic wand that could turn all the hill people into scheduled tribes. It was a long and complicated process that required ratification from the tribal welfare ministry. The draft agreement of the proposed Sixth Schedule status had spelled this out clearly: only those hill communities with proven tribal identities would get recognition.

But how could different communities vouch for their roots decades after they had left their ancestral villages in different parts of the Himalayas? Not only had they left behind their language and culture, but had formed a new community through intermarriages and by adapting to a cosmopolitan lifestyle in Darjeeling. This was as absurd as ordering a mountain spring to go back to its source.

I came back to the town of my memories to find the return-to-roots project in full swing. The familiar image of Goddess Durga had been banished to make way for stones. The study of dying languages, the conservation of old scripts, the revival of primitive rituals involving witch doctors and the celebration of ethnic foods, hooch and attire were being set off with great fanfare. Also, organizations of different communities like the Tamang, Rai and Kami had either been born, or had stirred from sleep.

This was altogether a surreal phenomenon that was unfolding under the contrary pulls of globalization and ethnic politics.

Before he cast himself into the firebrand rebel leader dressed in his trademark jacket and tie, Subash Ghising had tried his hand at writing romantic novels. Now he began to write the fiction of identity-construction in pure magic realist style.

∼

There is no deeper quicksand on earth than a return to the town of memories. No greater desert too. When I was still working here, Pratibha Datta had suffered a fall in her flat and broken a femur. Her age had ruled out surgery, and she had spent the final months of her life bedridden and under the care of nurses. She had died of septicaemia from a bedsore. Now I learnt that Animesh-da's father, too, had died. I went to St Joseph's College in search of Benson, only to be told that he had left the job and returned to Kerala. I would learn about his tragedy later. The quiet little guest house on Zakir Hussain Road had changed hands and had grown into a busy hotel. Most of my colleagues at the government college had either been transferred or had retired. Hemraj had moved to the US on a postdoctoral fellowship. Mother Damien of Loreto College had gone back to Dublin, her hometown. The watering hole behind the stable at Chowrasta, where Benson and I used to wash down plates of pork chips with cheap Sikkimese brandy, had metamorphosed into a restaurant. The apartment in Haridas Hatta where I had lived as a tenant was painted a bilious green; a number of buildings had come up around it. On the tiny balcony of the flat that used to be mine, where I had woven gossamers of melancholy on many a torpid afternoon, a burly woman was hanging out washing and prattling to an invisible child. The amiable old grocer at the corner store was no more. The street dogs, too, had changed. Most of the rooftops had sprouted dish antennas.

A return to the city of memories is like masturbation; the mating with memories goes on inside the head. It is followed by the ache of self-deception and guilt.

One day, I went to Jalapahar to call on Newton. As I was trying to recall how the place had been twenty years ago, I remembered a description of it in the early-twentieth-century book by Dozey: thick forests, the songs of cicadas, the green sheds of the military sanatorium lost in fog.

The porch of the house was now fitted with a grill and the floors were covered with marble, yet it had a look of neglect. Newton's mother came to answer the doorbell; she had bags under her eyes. His sister had married and lived in Gangtok now. His father's practice at the court had been curbed following a heart attack. A photograph of the great-grandmother, a digital print with garlands of plastic flowers, stood on top of the glass cabinet in the drawing room. Inside, the antique copper vessels had more bric-a-brac for company. But the photograph of the aunt and her Australian husband was missing. Instead, she herself was around. But the matronly lady was a far cry from the bubbly young girl in the photograph who had stood arm- in-arm with her husband before the Sydney Opera House.

She'd had a divorce and now ran a coffee shop on Hermitage Road. Newton sat at the counter occasionally, when he could squeeze time from his busy engagement with music. He had set up a rock band with a few friends; it was named Darjeeling Express. He was also keeping his hair long. After all these years, his mother's anxious pleas to me hadn't changed: 'You please give him good advice, sir.'

I took leave of them and walked along Gandhi Road.

Newton was with me. He was taking me to their recording studio, an abandoned video hall near Bethany School where members of his group were rehearsing. Darjeeling Carnival was a few weeks away and they were participating in it for the first time.

'How long do you plan to go on like this, Newton?' I asked him affably. 'Won't you find a job?'

'But where is the job, sir?' Newton asked me with a shrug. His ponytailed hair brushed against his neck. 'All the hotels and business establishments here are owned by people from the plains. Only the dishwasher's job is available.'

'Do you think a Sixth Schedule status will change this?' I asked.

'Change what?' Newton asked back testily. 'Now around thirty per cent of the people in Darjeeling are scheduled tribes. What will change if it becomes a hundred per cent? Nothing, unless new jobs are created.'

'But will Gorkhaland solve the problem?' I persisted. 'Biharis still have all the power in Jharkhand. In Uttarakhand, too, the Garhwalis have remained backward.'

Newton laughed. 'Now you are speaking like the British, sir. They used to give these arguments during the freedom movement, now the CPM is repeating them. Let Gorkhaland come, we'll manage these problems on our own.'

We were walking down the pavement of Mahakal Market. A flock of young well-dressed girls crossed the road. Newton watched them out of the corner of his eye.

'Are there girls in your band?' I asked him. 'No sir, all boys. Hundred per cent!' Newton laughed again.

'Don't you have a girlfriend?'

He fell silent for a moment, pulled his ponytail across the shoulder and began to straighten it.

'There was, but not any more. She was a friend's sister, a teacher in St Teresa's School. Now she is in Kolkata, training to become an airhostess. She used to teach English to little children, now she will serve napkins in the skies. Service sector!'

Newton laughed bitterly.

We reached the rehearsal room of Darjeeling Express. It was a big tin shed, covered on all sides, with rough wooden planks laid on the floor. Until a few years ago, it used to be a video hall to which the town's porters and labourers would flock. It had been turned into a sound-recording studio with musical equipment and cables strewn on the floor. Blocks of thermocol were laid over the walls and even the ceiling. Large posters of Western pop singers were pinned on them.

But, strangely, the music that filled the room was far from the ear-splitting heavy metal I was expecting. It was pure Nepali folk – very artless and very bucolic. A pair of rustic men in shapeless jackets and pajamas were beating small drums hanging from their necks and dancing in a slow rhythm. Three smart, well-dressed members of the band were trying to mimic their beats and movements. The two men came from a village in Nepal every year to work as porters during the tourist season.

'We are producing a video album,' Newton informed me. 'The title will be *Wings of the Root*.'

But of course the porters would not appear in the final album. The three band members would dress up in ethnic outfits and play the drummers. It was a sponsored project, funded by a local ethnic organization. The album would be sent to the tribal welfare ministry in New Delhi as proof of the tribal identity of a particular community. Darjeeling Express had produced two similar albums in the last few months. The payments were good.

'How is the title of the album, sir? Do you like it?' Newton asked.

Wings of the Root. A smart title, surely. But...

Newton noticed the haze on my face and assured me that there was nothing odd about this. Some community organizations were even sending camera crews to remote areas in Nepal to search out and record lost cultural roots.

I watched the spectacle of two ragged porters and three smart young men beating drums and stamping feet. A fog of anxiety began to rise in my mind. A wonderful human tapestry had been woven here for one and a half centuries, since Darjeeling was established, with coloured strands of diverse castes, creeds and ethnicities. Six decades after the British had left, after all the ravages of communalism and divisive politics in other parts of the country, this tapestry had remained unscathed. Even during the dark, violent days of the agitation in the 1980s, not a single drop of blood had been shed in the name of language and ethnicity. Surely, as everywhere, there were subterranean currents of grudges and mistrust flowing between the communities. They mostly stemmed from relative economic fortunes and proximity to power. But never had I seen these things create a fissure in hill society. If I were asked to make a list of my most precious memories of Darjeeling, I would put on top not the sunrise over Kanchenjunga, but the symphony made out of the muezzin's calls, the ringing of church and temple bells, and the blasts of Tibetan horns coming from different parts of the town at all hours of the day.

Now it seemed the symphony could fall silent any day, the rich tapestry could come apart.

Diverse roots had grown entwined for so long in the depths of the earth. What if they grew wings and wanted to break free of one another? Rivers of blood would flow. I couldn't share my thoughts with Newton that day but I left Darjeeling with dark forebodings. Soon, the darkness in my mind was blown apart by a fantastic uprising.

~

Subash Ghising had called the hill people to exhibit their tribal identities before the world by organizing stone-worship and hooch-drinking sessions as well as shaman dances. In the summer of 2007, the youth of the Darjeeling hills woke up to the call as a tribe, but in a manner contrary to anything Ghising could have imagined. The totem of this tribe was no vermilion-marked stone or animal figure, it was a young man named Prashant Tamang, a constable working with the Kolkata Police. Their rituals, too, didn't have drums, skulls or fire dances; rather, they involved satellite telecast, MP3 technology, broadband internet and mobile networks. The uprising was triggered by the competition programme *Indian Idol*, loosely based on the British programme *Pop Idol*, on a national television channel. For weeks, men and women in the Darjeeling hills and neighbouring Sikkim – indeed all over Northeast India – voted for the contestant Prashant Tamang through SMS and got him to win the title.

This created a history of sorts. Here was an unknown Gorkha boy suddenly becoming a household name across the country, not with the aid of a gun or a bomb, nor for military pluck or menial fealty, but for singing popular songs from Hindi movies. He garnered the overwhelming support of the hill people.

There was a growing consumer market across this hill region. But, except for footballer Bhaichung Bhutia, there was no popular local face that could be used in advertisements, one with whom the hill youth could identify. In Prashant Tamang, the market found that new face, it found a new icon.

But with the invention of an icon, a fascinating movement was set off in the hills. In one of the episodes of the programme, when Prashant was made to dress up like and mimic a Gorkha chowkidar in a Hindi film and sing the song, it sparked outrage in the hills. His supporters felt humiliated and came out on the streets to protest against the mindset, popular in North Indian cities, where a Gorkha and a watchman are interchangeable. The morning after he won the title, a presenter in a New Delhi FM radio channel cracked an offhand joke that since a Gorkha had become the Indian Idol, cases of burglary would rise in the city. The comment set off a mob of frenzied hill youth rampaging through the streets of Siliguri. The army had to be called out.

The plains of West Bengal were then caught in a spiral of political violence. Many lives had been lost in the western district of Jangalmahal and Nandigram. But the army was never needed there.

The army was called out again a few months later that year, on 21 November, in the heart of Kolkata. On that day, a group of young protesters from the local Urdu-speaking Muslim community suddenly became frenzied and rampaged through the streets and torched vehicles in the Ripon Street–Park Circus area; they were demanding the deportation of Bangladeshi writer Taslima Nasreen. Nobody had been attacked or injured, though. It seemed the then state administration resorted to this distress alarm when they were clueless about their perceived adversary, when they felt they were dealing with the proverbial Other. That Other could inhabit the hilly margin of the state, or a pocket inside the state capital.

A large number of men of Gorkha or Nepali origin work as chowkidars in different parts of India. This is as plain a fact as the large number of Sikhs who could be seen driving taxis and trucks a couple of decades ago. Countless films, advertisements and jokes harped on this stereotype. But did this ever anger the Sikhs? The Hindi movie *Padosan*, of timeless popular appeal, spins out a triangular love story involving a chic urban girl, a North Indian yokel and a clownish Tamil Brahmin. Did it spark off a civil war? Then why would the people of the Darjeeling hills flare up in anger if a Gorkha is jokingly called chowkidar?

The distance by road between Kolkata and Darjeeling is 623 kilometres. The distance, in terms of the mind, is 623 light years. Nobody made an effort to find out what had happened in the hills, and why. Nobody gave a thought to the fact that a young urban generation was emerging in the hill towns of the Darjeeling district. It was raring to break out of the stifling, century-old stereotype of a happy-go-lucky community and join the country's mainstream. A section of them were well-off, educated and conscious of their rights. They wanted to set sail upon the high tide of globalization which was then flooding all corners of urban life. They were adept at the language of the internet, of blogs and chats. Averse to the grime of party politics, a group in Darjeeling had set up a cultural organization named Darjeeling Initiative. It organized an annual programme, the Darjeeling Carnival, at Chowrasta. The week-long programme drew not only the youth of the Darjeeling hills, but even those living in other parts of the country. Some of them worked in BPOs and call centres in Gurgaon, Hyderabad or Bangalore, but were in close contact with their home in the hills. The aspiration of this new social group shaped up as the contest for the title of *Indian Idol* went on air, where a Darjeeling-ko-chora was winning the hearts of viewers across the country by singing songs that were truly pan-Indian – songs from popular Hindi movies.

The vehicle of aspiration was ready, it just needed someone bold and brash to slip behind the steering wheel. Bimal Gurung, a forty-something former taxi driver and a dissident municipal councillor from Ghising's party, chipped in. He revved up the engine by setting up Prashant Tamang fan clubs and raising subscriptions to open roadside phone kiosks so that the local youth could vote for their idol in the thousands by sending SMSes. The fever had caught on. Now he steered the vehicle on a collision course against his former mentor Subash Ghising. Destination: Gorkhaland.

The Latin origin of the word destination is *destinatio*, which means appointment. Between 1906 and 1986, an appointment was sought, and missed, twenty-five times. The Hillmen's Association and, since 1943, the All Bengal Gorkha League had been the most persistent. Even the Communist Party of India had wanted, in 1947, a separate state named Gorkhastan to be carved out of Sikkim, Nepal (both sovereign states then) and joined with the Darjeeling hills.

So this vehicle of aspiration was an old one, older than the vintage Land Rovers of Darjeeling but, like them, surprisingly sturdy and roadworthy. It began to trundle on again along the twisting, precipitous path of a political agitation. A motley crowd was riding it, including students, women, hunger strikers carrying portraits of Mahatma Gandhi, and also a scattering of mischief mongers – as always happens in the public transport of a mass movement. Blowing the horn and raising dust, the vehicle of youthful aspiration danced along bumpy hill paths.

No path in Darjeeling is straight, and sometimes it veered towards vertiginous khuds. However, an incredible journey had begun that continued through the long winter months. The bandhs, hunger strikes and daily protest marches gave way to novel forms of defiance, like people keeping themselves indoors in a self-imposed curfew. However, by spring of the following year, 2008, it became apparent that the movement was leading to another labyrinth. The destination had eluded everyone again, the appointment had been missed.

But an important mission had been achieved. Darjeeling's unique demographic tapestry, made out of diverse ethnic strands, had been spared. The hill people had emphatically rejected the Sixth Schedule, a constitutional safeguard designed to protect remote tribes who still clung on to ancient ways of life. Subash Ghising had wanted to turn the clock back by bringing around stone worship, shaman dances and other primitive rituals. Darjeelingeys didn't go back. Rather, it was Ghising himself who was consigned to the past.

His fall came swiftly, and caught everyone by surprise; though not a single bullet was fired, not a drop of blood was shed. In February 2008, he left for New Delhi to attend a meeting on the Sixth Schedule. He couldn't come back to Darjeeling again. The man without whose command the springs wouldn't flow, the clouds wouldn't drift, the birds wouldn't sing and even the sun wouldn't rise over Tiger Hill, was made to sign his resignation letter at a place on the outskirts of Siliguri, under heavy police security to protect him from his own people. At that very moment in Darjeeling, a jubilant crowd broke open the heavy iron gates of Lal Kothi, the headquarters of the Hill Council that had once been the summer palace of the Maharaja of Cooch Behar. Everyone rushed to the spot which, for two decades, had been the nerve centre of power in the hills – the plush, teak-panelled room adorned with imported rosewood furniture, crystal images of Goddess Chamunda, and a large map of the world: the official chamber of Chairman Saab.

∼

Now the news from Darjeeling reached me piecemeal via newspapers and television. But what a Darjeeling! Houses burning, streets strewn with broken glass, Glenary's vandalized. As I watched young men and women milling about dressed in regulation ethnic dresses on television, I mistook Darjeeling for an obscure Northeastern hill town. The famous smiles had vanished, leaving behind stiffened faces. It was not the town I had known.

But friends kept sending reassuring messages. Darjeeling was as she had always been, they wrote, only she was passing through difficult times. They wrote about the iron resolve of young people to fight for their collective dream, about couples who had pledged to put off marriage, about men who had pledged to go barefoot, and to give up alcohol, until they got Gorkhaland. On 5th September, Teachers' Day, I received the usual greetings and messages from some of my former students. One of them wrote, 'See you soon, sir, in the new dawn of Gorkhaland!'

Surely I'd be there, I told myself, in the new dawn. But would that dawn be as stupefying as my first at Hotel Sunshine's window, with streaks of pink light and a strange squeal coming from the butcher shop downstairs? That time I had failed to find the town of my grandfather's nostalgia. Would I find the town of my memories?

Guns and grenades were used during the agitation in the 1980s; its twenty-first-century avatar saw a more lethal weapon: black paint. Faces were being painted with it if anyone failed to obey the diktat and wear ethnic dresses.

Be it a chapter of history or a signboard, anything unwelcome can be easily covered over with black paint. Man's multiple identities can be screened by wielding the paintbrush. Amartya Sen has called this act the miniaturization of human beings. A propensity to miniaturize human beings by giving offensive names to people from different regions in the country was wired into the middle-class Bengali culture I belonged to. Perhaps I, too, would have been accustomed to this attitude had I not spent some of the best years of my life in Darjeeling. But now I had lost that angle of vision which refused to see the trees for the forest. So, when a friend in Kolkata casually remarked, 'All Gorkhas in Darjeeling are infiltrators, only the Lepchas are the true sons of the soil,' the face of Newton's great-grandmother came to my mind.

Someone else would comment: 'How can we give them a separate state? There is Nepal on one side and China on the other. What about the country's security?'

What would remain unsaid is the seed of suspicion about the Indianness of the people of Nepalese origin living in Darjeeling.

Did this seed grow roots in the dark depths of memories? Did it remind them of Ghising's call for a separate nation two decades ago and his appeal to the International Court of Justice? Or did the roots go deeper into the memory of the black day at Jallianwala Bagh, of the impassive faces of Gorkha infantrymen ranged in position?

~

My memories go back to a bend – not in time or history, but in a road, the Hill Cart Road. All first-time travellers to Darjeeling lose a heartbeat on this bend. Some even exclaim, 'Ah, Darjeeling!' It is from here that the town glides into view for the first time around a spur. On clear days the Kanchenjunga towers majestically in the background. Countless times have I seen from this bend the town of Darjeeling flutter up from the fold of the mountain like a pigeon from a magician's hat. Draped in sheer mist or awash in sunlight, it always evoked awe, and a mild shock. Sometimes it appeared like urban detritus dumped on the hillside, a volcanic eruption frozen in time, or even a biblical vision seen by the unknown medieval poet of 'Pearl':

> From a hill I spied
> That city, as onward still I sped:
> On the far side of the stream low laid
> Brighter than blazing sun it shone,
> As in the Apocalypse we read
> Described by the Apostle John

The view from that particular bend in the road affects everyone. I have seen various expressions play on the tired faces of Darjeelingeys returning after a sojourn in the plains, or some routine work in Siliguri. How did Sainlo of Halesi feel when he first glimpsed his dream town from this spot? How did Dadu and Julia feel when they passed it?

The place is known as Batasia. The famous loop on the Darjeeling Himalayan Railway is here, where the track spirals around itself through a tunnel and over a hilltop. There is no other spot in Darjeeling from where so many photographs of the town have been taken, the snow range of Kanchenjunga and the toy trains. Here the up-train halts for ten minutes on the last leg of its long journey from the plains. The tourists alight, take out their cameras, the children run around in the park, young couples saunter hand in hand away from the crowd.

And in this noisy, colourful concourse, on a raised circular platform, stands the tall bronze statue of a Gorkha soldier with a downcast face. Before him is a huge granite obelisk that can be viewed with the naked eye from the town on clear days. Carved on its sides are the names of 131 Gorkha soldiers who died as martyrs between 1947 and 2007. What is not written on the stone is the fact that of all the soldiers who lost their lives fighting wars and internal conflicts since Independence, the representation from the three hill subdivisions of Darjeeling district is the highest in the country.

Were they outsiders or secessionists? I shall never know.

~

So I'm asking who do you belong to?
I'm sure it's not yourself
Who do you sing love songs to?

~

Surely Darjeeling will find the answer one day. Or perhaps it never will. Perhaps the answer will be forever deferred. Meanwhile, new generations will come, full of restless anger; their impatience will be matched by the intolerance of the political establishment of Kolkata. No party with a support base in the plains of West Bengal can dare engage with the statehood demand of the hill people – that will amount to political hara-kiri.

The sentiment of the middle-class Bengalis about Darjeeling runs deep. After the colonial Bengal Presidency shrank and the country's capital was shifted to Delhi, after Partition rent Bengal into two and Calcutta slid from being the commercial hub of the country to a provincial city, much of the bhadralok Bengali's material and cultural capital was lost. Darjeeling was the last straw. It had big investments of nostalgia.

Any attempt to take off the blinkers of nostalgia, and see with candid eyes the possibility of a separate state comprising the three hill subdivisions of Darjeeling district and parts of Dooars, is bound to be contentious. While the proponents of Gorkhaland harp on Darjeeling's tea, tourism and hydel-power potential, and its opportunities in international border trade, the detractors point to its small size, topographic obstacles and limited scope for revenue to make it a viable state.

Emotions often follow a logic that hardcore economics cannot explain. On a television news broadcast, I heard a senior hill leader compare the demand for a separate state to be carved out of West Bengal with the crisis in a joint family. 'Little brother has now grown up and wants to set up his own family,' he said. 'Let the big brother pave the way.' A joint family can never be saved from break-up by warning the little brother of the material consequences of leaving the big brother.

But what if the big brother could speak in a different voice?

Brother, I need you. Don't go away. I need you, not because of your resources, your timber, tea and tourism. But I just need you by my side, for what you are. I need you because of your beauty, your rich cosmopolitan culture. If you leave me, I will become so dull and flat, you see, literally so, and so destitute of romance. Come, let's forget the past. Come, don't stand outside the door, in the watch-shed. Come inside, come to my heart.

What if the big brother could speak these words?

But big brothers never speak this language. Everywhere they speak the language of arrogance and the penal code, of missiles and fighter aircrafts. At the very least, they speak the language of lathi and tear gas.

On 9 April 2008, there was a lathicharge by the police on a peaceful procession of Gorkha army veterans on the outskirts of Siliguri town. They were demanding the separate state of Gorkhaland. The following day, I opened my internet mailbox to find the photographs that a friend from Darjeeling had sent: policemen in riot gear dragging away ex-soldiers with medals on their chests. The venerable old men had their shirts torn and their faces dazed with shock; many had wounds on their brows, from which blood had dripped on the medals. My friend wrote to me:

> We don't have a Saurav Ganguly, neither do we have an Amartya Sen. These veteran soldiers are the true idols in our society, as respected as our parents. Sitting in Kolkata, you people shall never understand the wounds these photographs have inflicted on the minds of the people here. A government decorates a hero with a medal for shedding blood for the country; another elected government spills the same blood on those very medals. Let us hope that the new state that will be born one day at the cost of this blood, shall never desecrate the medal of a soldier.

I don't know if that state will ever be born, what price in blood will be paid for it, or what its shape will be. But I do hope that the wounds in the minds of the hill people will heal one day. I hope untarnished medals will hang on the chests of proud soldiers, that every household in the hills will have enough food and water, I hope there will be teachers in schools and medicines in hospitals, I hope that electricity will at last come to the creeper-covered poles in Tuia, that Guiyes will receive old-age pensions, that the green women of Chowk Bazaar will have their own self-help groups, I hope the tea gardens will get back their health, that the cinchona farms in Mongpu will be revived, the sex workers will be rehabilitated. I hope the salamanders will procreate, the rickety horses on Chowrasta will get a veterinary hospital, the porters of Chowk Bazaar a TB clinic. I hope Pemba's ancestral umbrella will remain intact, and an archive will be set up in Darjeeling for vanishing manuscripts and artefacts, that forgotten Hope Town will be resurrected again. I hope the cancerous growth of Darjeeling will be stopped, the concrete structures around natural springs will be demolished. I hope Kaley's family will have savings for a rainy day, and every borough shall have a landslide-victims' shelter and a rehab clinic for drug addicts and scarecrows, and a university of technology in the hills. I hope Animesh-da's next generation will have a safe home in Darjeeling, and the rare orchids will have their home in the trees. I hope Louis Mandelli's lost birds will return to them, and Newton's girlfriend will come back to Darjeeling.

So many hopes, will they ever be fulfilled? I have no idea. I have only memories. As I delve into them, my last afternoon in Darjeeling drifts back.

~

It is a dark tin shed, an abandoned video hall. Two Nepalese porters are dancing to the beats of a drum. Three young men are mimicking their movements. A simple languid tune is rising to a crescendo and then dying. Now the five men are dancing together round and round, clapping their hands above their heads and swaying their hips. The rustic men are rheumy-eyed, with stubble on their chins, dressed in worn jackets and pajamas. The three husky young men are wearing jeans, T-shirts and ear studs. I turn to the faces of the two porters and notice that they are grim, and without a trace of the ardour that is animating their limbs. It seems they have lent their hands and feet to Newton and his friends, but their shoulders are still burdened with invisible loads.

The drums continue to reverberate in my ears long after they have stopped. Kiran-daju, the owner of the Zakir Hussain Road guesthouse, once told me that they had learnt to accurately guess an agitator, a policeman and a CRPF jawan from the sound of their footsteps. Those were the tense days of agitation. 'We could see with our ears,' he had said. I cannot see with my ears, but the relentless drums keep beating inside my head.

As I step out of the dark video hall, my eyes are dazzled. Nehru Road is flooded with a brilliant sun pouring through a gash in the clouds. In the pure rain-washed light, a crowd of colourfully dressed people have turned out like butterflies. The way to Chowrasta has become a veritable fairground, buzzing with laughter, chatter and the calls of peddlers. Sprays of soap bubbles are wafting in the air and sticking to the balaclavas of Bengali tourists; a young Western backpacker overtakes them with long strides; a pair of schoolboys, their arms round each other's necks, titter as they ramble about; three black-robed advocates strike up a conversation in the middle of the road; a baby girl riding her father's shoulders cradles his head with one hand and holds a melting ice-cream bar in the other; a petite, long-haired young girl in a midnight-blue miniskirt walks her dog, a brown labrador, along the pavement...

Limpid watercolours of Darjeeling, soon to be wiped out by the fog. But this evanescent moment is the town's most lasting memorial, for in it are caught its past, present and future.

NOTES

HOME WEATHER

1. Lady Betty Balfour, *The History of Lord Lytton's Indian Administration, 1876 to 1880: Compiled from Letters and Official Papers* (London: Longmans, Green and Co., 1899), p. 220.
2. Fred Pinn, *L. Mandelli (1833-1880): Darjeeling Tea Planter and Ornithologist* (London: Oxford University Press, 1985), p. 17.
3. Ibid.
4. Indra Bahadur Rai, 'The Storm Raged All Night Long', in *An Anthology of Nepali Short Stories in English*, ed., Bhanu Chhetri and Mangal S. Subba (Darjeeling: Munal Prakashan, 1999), p. 39.
5. Percy Brown, *Tours in Sikkim and the Darjeeling District* (Calcutta: W. Newman & Co., 1917), p. 4.
6. Indra Sundas, 'The Cartman', in *An Anthology of Nepali Short Stories in English*, ed., Chhetri and Subba, p. 30.

DAWN AT THE BUTCHER SHOP

1. L.S.S. O'Malley, *Bengal District Gazetteers: Darjeeling* (New Delhi: Logos Press, 1999), p. 110.
2. Laurence Fleming, ed., *Last Children of the Raj: British Childhoods in India 1939–1950 (Vol. 2)* (London: Radcliffe Press, 2004), p. 87.

SALAMANDERLAND

1. Quoted in H.V. Bayley, *Dorjé-ling* (Calcutta: G.H. Huttmann, Bengal Military Orphan Press, 1838), p. 50.

2. John Cameron Lowrie, *Two Years in Upper India* (New York: R. Carter and Brothers, 1850), p. 221.
3. Fred Pinn, *The Road of Destiny: Darjeeling Letters, 1839* (New Delhi: Oxford University Press, 1987), p. 165.
4. Ibid., p. 42.
5. Frederick Marshman Bailey, *No Passport to Tibet* (London: Rupert Hart-Davis, 1957), p. 45.
6. William Brook Northey, *The Land of the Gurkhas, or The Himalayan Kingdom of Nepal* (Cambridge: W. Heffer & Sons Ltd, 1937), p. 211.
7. Dane Kennedy, *The Magic Mountains: Hill Stations and the British Raj* (Berkeley: University of California Press, 1996), p. 10.
8. Niraj Lama, 'Chowrasta Chatter', *The Statesman*, 25 December 2005.

GUIYE AND THE SCARECROWS

1. Andrew Robinson, *Satyajit Ray: The Inner Eye. The Biography of a Master Film-Maker* (New York: I.B. Tauris, 2004), p. 139.
2. E.C. Dozey, *A Concise History of Darjeeling District Since 1835: With a Complete Itinerary of Tours in Sikkim and the District* (Calcutta: Jetsun Publishing House, 1989), p. 47.
3. Ibid., p. 125.
4. Laurence Fleming, ed., *Last Children of the Raj: British Childhoods in India 1939–1950 (Vol. 2)* (London: Radcliffe Press, 2004), p. 8.
5. Ibid., p. 9.
6. Laurence Fleming, ed., *Last Children of the Raj: British Childhoods in India 1919-1939 (Vol. 1)* (London: Radcliffe Press, 2004), p. 252.
7. William Brook Northey, *The Land of the Gurkhas, or The Himalayan Kingdom of Nepal* (Cambridge: W. Heffer & Sons Ltd, 1937), p. 220.

PEMBA'S UMBRELLA

1. David Crystal, *Language Death* (Cambridge: Cambridge University Press, 2000), p. 4.

2. Laurence Austine Waddell, *Among the Himalayas* (Cambridge: Cambridge University Press, 2015), p. 293.
3. Fred Pinn, *The Road of Destiny: Darjeeling Letters, 1839* (New Delhi: Oxford University Press, 1987), p. 87.
4. Waddell, *Among the Himalayas*, p. 73.
5. L.S.S. O'Malley, *Bengal District Gazetteers: Darjeeling* (New Delhi: Logos Press, 1999), p. 54.
6. Geoffrey Gorer, *Himalayan Village: An Account of the Lepchas of Sikkim* (London: Nelson, 1967), p. 151.
7. Ibid., p. 161.

ABOUT THE AUTHOR

Parimal Bhattacharya, a bilingual writer and translator, is an associate professor of English in the West Bengal Education Service. He is the author of *Bells of Shangri-La* and *Field Notes from a Waterborne Land*. *Nahumer Gram O Onyanyo Museum*, published in 2021, is his most recent work in Bangla.

30 Years *of*
HarperCollins *Publishers* India

At HarperCollins, we believe in telling the best stories and finding the widest possible readership for our books in every format possible. We started publishing 30 years ago; a great deal has changed since then, but what has remained constant is the passion with which our authors write their books, the love with which readers receive them, and the sheer joy and excitement that we as publishers feel in being a part of the publishing process.

Over the years, we've had the pleasure of publishing some of the finest writing from the subcontinent and around the world, and some of the biggest bestsellers in India's publishing history. Our books and authors have won a phenomenal range of awards, and we ourselves have been named Publisher of the Year the greatest number of times. But nothing has meant more to us than the fact that millions of people have read the books we published, and somewhere, a book of ours might have made a difference.

As we step into our fourth decade, we go back to that one word – a word which has been a driving force for us all these years.

Read.

Harper Collins   4th   HARPER PERENNIAL   HARPER BUSINESS   HARPER BLACK   हार्पर हिन्दी

HarperCollins *Children's Books*   HARPER DESIGN   HARPER VANTAGE   Harper Sport